Color it Home

Color it

A Builder's Guide to

Beverly Trupp

CBI Publishing Company, Inc.
51 Sleeper Street
Boston, Massachusetts 02210

Home

Interior Design and Merchandising

Library of Congress Cataloging in Publication Data

Trupp, Beverly
Color it home.

1. Model houses.   2. Interior decoration.
II. Title.
NK2195.M6L56   747.213   80-25302
ISBN 0-8436-0137-X

Printed in the United States of America

Printing (last digit): 9 8 7 6 5 4 3 2 1

Contents

Preface

A Word of Thanks . . .

Chapter 1. Don't Decorate It; Merchandise It   **1**
Here are the five basic rules on how to merchandise model homes effectively.

Chapter 2. Know Thy Market   **11**
If you want to get the most out of your merchandising program, you have to know how to create a lived-in look and sell those extra bedrooms!

Chapter 3. The Psychology of Color   **23**
Color can put prospects in the right 'buying' moods. To learn about color's persuasive powers, read on.

Chapter 4. Putting Color to Work   **38**
When, where, why and how to use color for maximum effect is the sales message here.

Chapter 5. Architecture: If You've Got It, Flaunt It!   **53**
Architectural amenities are a model's most saleable features; here's how to make the most of them.

Chapter 6. Build Up Sales With Built-Ins   **61**
To build in or not to build-in? This chapter gives you a variety of reasons for adding built-ins to your merchandising package.

Chapter 7. The Nuts and Bolts   **76**
These are the bread and butter basics of merchandising. The mood-makers that set the stage for your sales story.

Chapter 8. Accessories: Those Special Touches   **91**
Learn how accessories communicate sales messages that elicit positive emotional response—and thus, sales.

Chapter 9. Create Male Spaces in All the Right Places   **105**
Use your most persuasive powers on the male side of the buying team by creating irresistible retreats that are just for HIM.

Chapter 10. Make the Kitchen Appetizing   **115**
A kitchen isn't just a place for cooking; it's a 'living room' that deserves a full course merchandising menu.

Chapter 11. Bathrooms: Make a Big Splash   **125**
Baths are today's showcase rooms; plenty of sizzle here can assure you sales.

Chapter 12. Design Small Spaces to Live Big   **134**
How to make prospects think "BIG" when floor space is diminishing.

Chapter 13. Add Some Fun Spots   **147**
Beauty is only skin deep. The model homes that sell are also "fun" places to be; a place to kick back and relax.

Chapter 14. Making the Most of Nostalgia   **157**
Conjure up memories and capture little truths from the past to make prospects feel at home; here's how.

Chapter 15. Sprucing Up the Sparkle   **171**
Get the most out of your merchandising dollar by keeping models in their prime right down the line.

Chapter 16. Working with the Interior Merchandiser   **184**
What to expect from the interior merchandiser when you decide to work with a pro.

Chapter 17. Get the Most Out of Your Merchandising Dollar   **193**
Learn how to spend your merchandising dollar to maximize your investment.

Chapter 18. The 'Model' Model   **198**
Some guidelines for those seeking perfection and bottom line profits.

Preface

When I first started thinking of this book about two years ago, I thought of it as information I could give to builders, developers, interior designers, architects, students and homemakers to help each more fully appreciate the joy of creating a personal home environment.

But something happened along the way. As I researched, wrote, talked to people and rewrote, I found I was the one on the receiving end.

After more than ten years in the business of merchandising model homes, the evolution of COLOR IT HOME has taught me new lessons and values, and has given me new insights I will treasure always.

My love and respect for the Builder—the farsighted men, and women, who spend years and years in the planning and building of "The American Dream"—is boundless.

The builder's instincts, I've found, are entrepreneurial. He is willing to take big risks to build our homes the way he believes we want them.

He is dynamic and decisive.

He is devoted to his life's purpose, and is seldom (if ever) deterred by the obstacles he encounters along the way—obstacles like a more and more restrictive public voice which, unwittenly hurts the very buyer it seeks to protect by ultimately increasing the cost of homes—obstacles like endless governmental red tape, labor strikes, material shortages, uncompromising weather conditions. And, yes, even temperamental architects and interior designers.

Often, this same builder is not so totally subjective when it comes to interior design and merchandising. Too often he is tempted to select his own favorite colors for carpeting, or to turn the whole job over to a secretary in the office. While these decisions may be fine for his own home, they are not the way to merchandise a model home—that is, to create a believable lifestyle for the target market.

So this book is primarily intended to assist the builder in this important aspect of his total marketing program.

I think you will find the thoughts and recommendations in COLOR IT HOME sound for years to come. Please use this book as a constant source of reference. Here are some ways you can make it work for you over and over again:

· Reread the book before you begin each new project. You will suddenly find completely different

messages as you think of your newest
project. Don't trust your memory to
relate these guidelines to every single
project in the same way.

· With this book you don't have to
hire professionals if budget prohibits.
Follow the guidelines in the book and
you will be ahead of the game.

I extend my deepest gratitude
to everyone who has helped make
this book possible, and particularly to
the Builder who has made my business of interior design so personally
fulfilling.

Love, *Bev*

A Word of Thanks . . .

Where do I begin expressing my appreciation for being part of this book? Yes this book is the result of a team of people's thoughts, love, patience, joy and commitment.

First I give the glory to God for bringing this to reality. And for using my friends to make this book into something beautiful we can share with you.

To David Link, the Editorial Director of Professional Builder magazine, for without him there would not be "Color It Home." He created the idea.

To Gail Stoorza and Peggy Walker who have sustained me and supported me throughout the writing of it.

To Tom Lewis who took all of it and wrapped it into the special package it is, keeping in mind my desire to keep it simple and somewhat child-like.

To all my clients who have allowed me to present our projects through the beautiful photography of Leeland Lee, Michael Muckley and Robb Miller.

And a giant hug and kiss to my staff at Color Design Art. Without their incredible support and constant challenging this would never have happened.

I salute: Don Anderson, my brother and loving friend who is also my partner. And my other partners, Frank Leo, the finest friend a person can ask for; and Jan Willeford whose loyalty, tenacity and professionalism has added quality to CDA's reputation. To Chuck and Yoli Landrum, truly the backbone of CDA; Pat Stone who watches over all of us so carefully; Kae Kleinman who makes everyday a joy; Kris Derdivanis whose thorough-ness makes working with her super; Peter Scantlebury who always has a beautiful, willing spirit; and of course Julie, Beverly, Jody, Terry and both of our Jennifer s whose beautiful attitudes and commitment to their work make CDA what it is today.

Last but not least, I must say a big "thank you" to the most precious Mom, a perfect "10" in my life whose example I am challenged to follow.

I love you and you are all a part of this book.

God bless you!

PS—I almost forgot my two furry friends, Kranker & Tootsie. You'll see Tootsie with me on the back jacket flap.

1

Don't Decorate It; Merchandise It.

You expect to hear oohs and aahs . . . but when you hear "this is me!" you know you've got a winner. You've colored it home.

What's the secret? What makes one builder's model home capture hearts and deposits when another of similar scope and plan does little to generate sales?

The answer is in merchandising. When a builder asks me whether to furnish a model home or not, I tell him: "Don't furnish it. Don't even decorate it. merchandise it!"

"Decorating" is a singular art, oriented to aesthetics.

"Merchandising", on the other hand, combines the creativity and know-how of design with sophisticated marketing techniques. Its function is to sell.

Certainly the interior design of a model home should be visually appealing. But

Model merchandising is more than decorating. It's setting the stage, and it begins right at the front door!

remember that personal taste and the way we perceive things vary as much as our personalities. Merchandising takes this into consideration by gearing the aesthetics of design to the types of people most likely to buy in the model home development.

It also takes into consideration the fact that good design alone is not enough to sell homes. A model home must be functional. It must be warm, inviting, comfortable and "livable" as well as visually stimulating. In other words, it should not only look good; it should "feel" good.

It's easy to spot the well-merchandised model. It has a sense of totality and excitement. Every room has been finished—from the smallest secondary bedroom to the main living areas—with furnishings, window treatment and accessories collectively coordinated to approximate the types of residence families within the target market would expect to own.

In total, it says to the buyer, "You could kick off your shoes and move right in." Why? Because the builder has accomplished three important objectives. He has:
- identified the target buyer;
- shown the function or purpose of what he has to sell
- and packaged it for optimum results in his identified market.

Those objectives are basic to good merchandising. And that's what this book is all about: Merchandising model homes as a sound investment.

Landscaping and sales offices both should set the mood of a model complex. Classic romanticism thrives in this sales office, themed around contemporary Victorian architecture.

Model landscaping cost about $120,000, and the money was effectively spent (photo left). Color Design Art of Santa Monica, Calif. designed the sales center at Heritage (photo below); it began as a standard two-car garage, but ended up as a sparkling reception area. Of special note: The stained glass skylight.

The Five Basic Rules Over the years I have come to believe strongly in what I've termed the "Five Basic Rules of Successful Merchandising." These are experience-proven rules you can apply to your own interior design strategy to make every model home an irrestible product. You will read these rules again and again in this book because these are the basic tools that can—and do—create sales. They are:

1. Know Thy Market
2. Wrap It
3. Theme It
4. Accessorize It
5. Color It

1 Let's take the first rule, KNOW THY MARKET. To the building professional, and to the interior designer or merchandising specialist who will assist him, it means you do your homework, your research.

Before you embark on the decorating—and what will likely be a substantial investment in thought, time and money—become acquainted with the market you hope to attract in your development.

What is the family's income? What does the head of the household do? Are there children and, if so, how many? Are they likely to be first-time owners or second or third-time buyers? What are their interests and hobbies likely to be, and how will they spend their time at home?

These are the kinds of questions you need to answer in order to create a home-like environment that will appeal to the tastes, lifestyles, incomes and expectations of the target market.

There's always more than one way to state a theme in order to achieve broader market appeal. In these two models nostalgia is expressed two ways. In the first, it's Hispanic to complement elements of classic Spanish architecture. (The gorgeous papier maché parrot is by the artist Bustamente).

Here nostalgia takes a Victorian twist. The development was aptly named "Heritage".

Just as important as determining a lifestyle "profile" of the target market is knowing what the "dream" aspirations of those people or families may be.

When people buy things—be it hot dogs, high fashion or housing in the suburbs—they want to think it will improve their lives and fulfill at least some of those "dream" expectations. That's part of the merchandising job—to give the buyer that touch of inspiration that his future will be better in the "dream" environment of the model home you create. Remember, it should be a dream house to be sure; but an achievable dream, not an impossible one!

Once you've determined the market—the most basic and important aspect of model home merchandising—you're ready for the creative aspects:

WRAP IT, the second rule, concerns the packaging of model homes. Just as we gift wrap a box to be exciting and festive, we "wrap" the model to excite and delight.

Wall coverings, floor coverings, window treatment and counter materials are the home's "gift wrappings" and can, depending on what is selected and how it is coordinated, create an infinite number of environments within the same floor plan or give a whole new life and look to furnishings.

2

Your merchandising plan should allot considerably more expense for attractive "wrappings" than might be provided in an ordinary decorating budget. That's because these background treatments are basic to the total impact of the model home setting. They comprise the background that sets the particular mood you intend to achieve and sell. And they help create favorable first impressions that will result in memorable lasting ones.

On the other hand, less may be spent on furnishings. The many extras of a merchandising program will eliminate the need for high-priced furniture that often calls more attention to itself than to the total environment.

In merchandising, we don't want people falling in love with the perfect chair or table or even the perfectly designed room. We want them to fall in love with the HOME. So we "wrap" it up to create love-at-first-sight kinds of feelings.

3 The third rule, THEME IT, is a merchandising technique built around a theme, or story, designed to sell.

Theming assures a very memorable model complex that wins hearts and fires imaginations because it targets appeal directly to the buyer market you have identified for your house or your development.

The secret of sure-fire theme merchandising is to know your market to the extent you know without a doubt the lifestyle "stories" with which it identifies. Then build your theme from there.

A well-executed theme should be the thread that unifies every aspect of the model or residential development and creates a saleable and unforgettable identity.

There are natural themes to be found in the surroundings of every project—a lake, the ocean, the history of the land that has been acquired—and in what you plan to provide such as a tennis club, golf courses, marina or equestrian facilities.

Theme stories can be carried through consistently from architecture and model decor to landscaping, marketing and advertising to relate the type of community you have developed.

On the other hand, themes can be used in individual decor within each home to create a variety of looks from model to model that will appeal to different tastes. One might be contemporary, the others Victorian, Colonial and Spanish. The idea behind theming is to establish a lifestyle image for your buyers.

The fourth rule, ACCES-SORIZE IT, is the frosting on the cake. There's no easier or more creative way to breathe personality into interiors than through accessorization.

These special touches are the kinds of things people will identify with when they walk in a room because they create the feeling that someone already lives in the home. They create a family atmosphere.

Accessories turn on buyer emotions because they make the merchandized model look as if someone genuinely cares; as if the builder went a little farther and wanted people to feel good when they came into the house.

The fifth rule, COLOR IT, also relates to the all important task of making people feel good. It is the most vital of all the merchandising techniques.

Color triggers the emotions. It can excite, soothe and motivate. But it can also disturb and agitate.

Every merchandiser needs to understand the importance of the impact of color on prospective home buyers. It plays, without a doubt, one of the most important roles in nature, our lives and in our perceptive processes.

I have always considered the use of color the very foundation of successful, sales-generating model home complex merchandising. And research has confirmed what I always felt intuitively about color: It is a means of communicating to would-be-buyers the kinds of messages that elicit positive emotional responses; the kinds that influence sales. In later chapters I'll talk about the results of market research into color and its effect on home-buyers.

For every lifestyle, there's a style for entertaining ... You can turn prospects onto it with accessories.

How The Dollar Is Spent. Merchandising. Wrapping. Theming. And Color! How much will all this cost? And does it cost more to "merchandise" a model than to "decorate" one? Not necessarily.

Merchandising budgets will vary per project and will be spent in different ways but need not be more expensive than decorating. Merchandising, in fact, is cost-effective when the home builder is familiar with the techniques that get him the utmost for his merchandising dollar. The chapter on budgeting, "Getting the Most Out of Your Merchandising Dollar," goes into explicit details on budgeting, where and how to spend your dollars, and where to cut back when need be. But for now, the important point to remember is this:

A well-planned merchandising program can—and should—stretch budget dollars without scrimping on impact by employing cost-saving approaches. These are things that are evident to the trained eye yet admired by the casual observer, techniques such as good use of colors or clever accessories. The same is true with a purposeful simplicity in interior design approaches that says less really can be more.

Most important, merchandising need not cost any more than decorating, but the end result will pay handsomely in better and faster home sales in your development, be it large or small, high-end or low, sophisticated townhomes in the city or family homes in the suburbs.

The following chapters of this book talk about the hows and whys of experience-proven merchandising techniques, all of them geared to saying "somebody will live a good life" in your model home whatever the style or price range.

Guidelines to a Well-Merchandised Model. Once you've put together your model merchandising plan, you may want to go over the following checklist. Ask yourself if your plan, when executed, will meet the criteria that can assure you a well merchandised product. If you read through this checklist and don't have all the answers, read on through this book. Then come back and rate your own merchandising programs.

1. Does your interior design/merchandising plan focus on a particular market? What are the demographics?

2. Have you researched and studied the market to the extent you know how members within the families are likely to spend their time at home and at leisure? List some of their likely activities, sports, hobbies:

3. Have you become familiar with the most likely submarkets within the target market income group? Will submarkets include young families, older ones, adults only, singles, professional couples, single couples, retirees?

4. Have you considered how you will wrap your model with appropriate wall, floor and surface coverings, window treatments and other "wrappings" to catch the eye of target buyers?

5. What about theme. Have you chosen an overall development theme? If so, how will each model home in the model complex support that theme in interior design? What about individual model themes. What are they, will they coordinate with each other and support the overall theme? List your major development theme and model sub themes:

_____

_____

_____

6. What color schemes have you chosen for your models? Does your design plan follow the color choice throughout each model home?

Are color themes coordinated from model to model? Are bold colors and soft colors bunched together or staggered for effect?

Draw a map of your model complex layout and identify the color scheme for each home.

7. Have you taken the current economy into consideration concerning color choices? Have you considered what kind of impact "polar" colors may have on your buyers?

8. Is there at least one "safe" color theme in one of your model designs?

9. Is your design package consistent with the price of the model home? That is, is the decorating cost within budget of a likely buyer candidate? Or have you gone overboard with design and furnishings too expensive for the home and the buyer?

10. Does your interior design/merchandising package come together to create impact on first impression? What are some of the items, colors, wrappings that the prospect will see first on entering your homes? List those items. Then ask yourself if those are things you want the eye to see first.

_____

_____

_____

11. Have you merchandised your model's strong points? Have you played up important architectural features, accentuated spaciousness and made the most of cozy corners?

List your models' most important strong points. Then ask yourself how those features might best be emphasized and merchandised.

_____

_____

12. Have you added character to the model with live plants and accessories you plan to use to describe lifestyle for the target market?

ROOM   ACCESSORIES

_____   _____

_____   _____

_____   _____

_____   _____

13. Have you included at least one memorable item in every model? Something to create lasting impact?

What and where?

_____

_____

14. Have you given each room a personality of its own? How? List special design features, accent points, accessories or built-in features.

_____

_____

15. Have you helped buyers visualize how to use space effectively with built-ins, special furniture arrangements and key placement of accessories?

16. Have you made the most of wide-open spaces yet retained a warm, human proportion? How?

17. Have you shown how your home will function? Where families will spend their time? How bedrooms, secondary bedrooms in particular, might function? What about family rooms, living areas and bonus rooms? Have you described how buyers might use them most effectively? Have you illustrated eating space in kitchens? If there is no dining room, have you demonstrated alternative dining place options?

18. Have you arranged furniture to facilitate convenient traffic flow?

19. Have you paid careful attention to smallest details? What about lighting, picture arrangements, accessories in pantries and closets? Are tables set for eating? Are yards attractive and patios merchandised?

20. Do you have a plan for keeping the model maintained in showcase condition? Write out your housekeeping and maintenance programs and distribute copies to salesmen or executives who will be in charge of follow-through.

21. Have you educated salesmen on the fine points of your models and your merchandising? Are they aware of the most important features of your homes? And, of the importance of their own positive attitudes in selling those homes?

2

Know Thy Market.

Somebody will live a good life in your model homes, to be sure, but who?

Successful model home merchandising begins with the "WHO" before it deals with the "HOW" of fabric and furnishings.

And the important "WHO" is the target market—the people who ultimately will live in the environments you create.

At the very beginning of your model house or development plan you should identify the most likely candidate buyers for your home, location and price range. Then get to KNOW THY MARKET well! I call this the "First Commandment" of model home merchandising.

Merchandising models is not self-indulged creativity. It's knowing that person/people/family out there who could and should buy your home, and designing interiors to meet their needs and desires.

People buy extra bedrooms when they're merchandised to reflect the lifestyle and hobbies of the target buyer.

There was a time when most model homes were simply "decorated" showcases with little regard for the needs, wants or lifestyles of the people who might live in them.

These "decorator's delights" were a great place for escape for Sunday afternoon browsing but could hardly be described as "liveable." In many cases they were overwhelming, even intimidating, leaving buyers no idea of how their own families might live in the home. Or any desire to do so.

In today's competitive market, however, it's not the interior "decor" but the life style you merchandise that will be your most important selling point. And when that life-style is geared directly to your market, it can:

· Create instant buyer identification.

· Woo prospects to "come in", "be comfortable" and feel "at home."

· Help them visualize their own belongings in the house.

· Project their own families in the new environment in their "own" rooms, doing the things they like best.

· Illustrate "achievable dream" environments that buyers can expect to easily duplicate for themselves.

This is what I mean by "comfortable". The room is sophisticated yet "homey"; not overdone. Prospects could visualize their own furnishings here.

Create A Lived-In Look. The most successful approach to merchandising lifestyles is creating what I call the "lived-in" look. It produces a "home" within the model home as if a family of similar tastes and abilities to that of the target market already resides within, and is very happy to be there, thank you!

You can adapt the approach easily to any home or development. You begin by developing a written profile of your prospective buyer—including his financial abilities, social and recreational preferences, family needs, current lifestyle, and that dream lifestyle which the family could realistically attain.

Then, based on that profile, you create a lifestyle decor within the model—or a series of lifestyles decors if it is a complex—that will compliment the achieveable dreams of your market population.

Remember that the end result should be "dream" homes to be sure, but plausible and achieveable dreams.

Don't portray the $80,000 property as a $150,000 property. You'll draw the wrong audience and ultimately turn off the potential customer with high-priced furnishings or decor beyond his budget.

On the other hand, if you're catering to a high-end market, those buyers understandably will look for elegance and custom design. So give them a full measure of luxury and lavish amenities.

Remember, the key to successful sales and profits lies with your market, and knowing what it wants, needs and expects.

Research: The Preliminary Priority. Research obviously is a priority in merchandising lifestyles geared to a specific market. It begins with demographics of the target buyers—i.e.; age, sex, family size, income, ages of children, recreational preferences, etc.

You'll want to determine some other statistics. For example, are those families likely to be first-time buyers or young marrieds? Empty nesters, professionals or a combination? And if so, including which submarkets? And you'll want to know how they like to spend their free time.

The time to size up your market is at the start of your project. By beginning early you can weave your merchandising scheme into every aspect of your model home development, from graphics on signs; overall theme and architectural design to the last accessorized detail inside.

You may want to retain a professional firm for your market analysis. Or, do it in-house, with the help of your development team—the architect, landscape designer, interior designer/merchandiser and other marketing or advertising professionals assisting you. The important tasks are to begin early and be thorough.

Tune In And Turn 'Em On. Many times builders can easily identify the market, but may not know just how to reach that market through interior merchandising.

It's really not so difficult if you get to know your market intimately. Little clues will help you communicate effectively.

You can read, watch and listen. Find out what books your market reads. And how they dress. What kind of movies and music appeal to those folks? What do their children do? How do they relax and play?

Become aware of what the market wants by visiting restaurants and stores—places where the target buyer is likely to eat, shop, play and be entertained. Look into sports and recreational opportunities.

Find out what current trends turn on your buyer and you'll know how to create a desire in that would-be owner's heart that makes him want your product.

By doing so, you'll find that this kind of marketing "homework" can help you relate your model home interiors to the targeted buyer in an honest, realistic way that makes prospects identify immediately with your homes.

Now the Fun Begins. Once you've established a thorough market profile, (a sample is illustrated) the real fun begins!

The next step is to draw up profiles of families who meet the criteria of the target market—then merchandise your models around those imaginary families. It's almost like writing a short story or play.

I draw up very detailed profiles (see the one on pages 16 and 17) so that it is clear exactly who we are designing the model home for and why. You'll learn from one of these profiles, for example, exactly what the head of household does for a living, how much he earns and how he spends his leisure time.

You'll learn how many children are in the family and what their ages are, how they like to play and how the mother spends her time.

Home shoppers browsing through the resulting model will marvel at an abundance of freshly watered plants, books ready for reading or tables set for entertaining and kids rooms that look like places for kids!

I believe in merchandising kitchens to be warm and habitable with pots and pans set out or other cooking paraphernalia. Potted herbs may be part of the decor. Also cookbooks, wall graphics and anything that says "this is a warm happy place to be; a special niche for someone who likes to cook!"

Family Rooms and Bedrooms also are key areas for merchandising the "lived-in" look. Living rooms are really "status" rooms that tell us how a family would like to live. In the family room, however, we discover how people live their daily lives.

Color Design Art

MARKETING INFORMATION:

This residential development is revolutionary in that design elements are fitted to the life of the affluent new homebuyer. New thinking in design was called for as an alternative to the traditional and typical products developed in past years in this growing Southern California market.

Marketing research indicated that the typical and traditional product is being rejected, even when larger square footage is involved, and that buyers seek better feature appointments including upgraded appliances, fixtures, etc.

The primary differences in this new product line—when related to the traditional and "tired" housing product—is the fact that each of the floorplans is targeted at a highly differentiated and identified target market, i.e., empty nesters, young professional couples, active families with older children, etc.

Here's a look at floorplans and targeted markets:

MODEL 1.

It has the most massive ceiling volume and interior special effects of any of the plans. Because of this spaciousness, the house needs to be decorated "down" so that the buyer can read the floorplan, configuration and room sizes. The family room in this plan relates to the formal area, and can be treated as an extension of the living room for large-scale entertaining. A bonus room upstairs can take the place of the traditional family room.

FAMILY PROFILES:

PROFILE 1

The family living in this home has a New England background. While the feeling of the home is traditional, they love the way the contemporary architecture displays some special furniture pieces that have been in the family for generations. He is a bank executive. She loves to cook and entertain for special occasions.

While the first floor has an adult orientation, the second floor is children's territory. The bonus room is designed for the kids and their friends. The bedroom of a 16-year-old daughter indicates she is a serious ballet dancer. Auto racing is one of the 10-year-old son's favorite sports, as indicated by accessories in a fourth bedroom.

MODEL 2.

This is the smallest plan, designed for empty nesters whose kids have left home. In this location, it will be purchased by affluent mature households moving out of large custom homes. These couples will desire a reallocation of interior living space away from a large family room, with the home taking on a more formal orientation. There is a major market in housing in this price range and size.

PROFILE 2

A semi-retired insurance agent and his wife live in this home which has a Country French feeling in furnishings. The "empty nesters" moved recently from a large custom home to smaller square footage since the last child is grown and married. They travel often, enjoy golf and like to weekend in the desert. When home they entertain frequently. She collects china, some of which is used at family holiday gatherings. Bedroom two is for visiting family or guests.

MODEL 3.

This home would suit a mature market or a family market, desiring one level living. The family room, which relates to the formal area, will again be treated as an extension of the living room to a degree. The kitchen is particularly large and suited to entertaining families who enjoy a well-stocked, well-designed kitchen.

PROFILE 3

This is the home of the youngest family. Her color sensitivity and eye for design is reflected in the tasteful design of the home, its romantic feeling and the art decor accents. She is the one friends and family call upon for decorating advice. He is an industrial real estate developer. The couple are both into gourmet cooking and like to entertain friends at dinner followed by an evening of bridge. Bedroom three has rabbits all around—their eight-year-old daughter's favorite animal. Boats are the theme in a six-year-old boy's room.

MODEL 4.

This was specifically designed for the young professional couple, probably without children, but in some cases young children. This buyer may be among the youngest, but possibly the most affluent and most avant garde in tastes. The excited interior volume of the plan will certainly attract this market specifically. The master bedroom is very private and separate.

4

PROFILE

The sophisticated use of natural fabrics and colors creates a contemporary feeling in this home. The professional couple who live here are trendsetters. They enjoy entertaining friends and associates but also view their home as a retreat from their very busy schedules. She is a fashion coordinator for a high-end department store chain. He owns an electronic parts manufacturing company. The den is his home office. He enjoys jogging every morning and they both play tennis, often entering weekend tournaments. Bedroom two is for guests, but doubles as her retreat.

MODEL 5.

With an elaborate and exciting entry hall treatment including a spiral staircase, is exceptionally elegant with a formal feeling. A sun room off the living room is a sitting room for guests who are very close to the family and will probably be utilized for backgammon and other activities shared only by the most intimate friends of the household. The home's spaciousness and formality call for decoration in a traditional look but with enough "revolutionary" looks to appeal to the sophisticated, affluent buyers in this income bracket.

5

PROFILE

This dramatic model is the home of an active established family. He is a stockbroker, educated in the East. They use the family room as a den/library. The formal living areas are used when they have larger gatherings; the sun room is for intimate family times together, or conversations with close friends. She volunteers time for charity functions, and often holds charity luncheons in her home. Their 14-year-old daugher loves horses and competes in English riding events. The 10-year-old son is a baseball nut as evidenced by the baseball memorabilia in his room—bedroom 3.

Family photos and sporting or hobby gear and a television set in this room say it's a family center. There may also be a game table with a backgammon set, open for family play. Bookshelves and built-ins might reveal favorite collections or antiques, or maybe a wine buff's corner.

As you progress into the bedrooms, individual personalities of family members should be identified.

· You learn from the stockpile of records, or stuffed animals in one bedroom, for example, that this is a teenager's retreat.

· Children's rooms abound with toys and the trappings of current fads—bicycling or roller skating equipment, for instance. (These obviously won't be the same interests of every prospective buyer's family, but they will be closely related and will identify the who might reside within).

· Master bedrooms give a feeling of residency with which both husband and wife can identify—a comfortable easy chair for reading, a desk for letter writing, a windowside table set for morning coffee and plenty of "his" or "her" accessories, that suggest a very personal, private retreat.

Everything Looks Homey. As you plan and budget for the "lived-in" look, keep in mind that it is a combination of care-fully selected "wrappings", such as floor and wall coverings that match the lifestyle of the target buyer, colors keyed to market preferences and current trends; and selected furnishings, as well as accessories, that produces the total effect.

You won't want expensive fur-nishings that take up a large chunk of the budget. A few "stunning" pieces lost in bare rooms won't create a lifestyle environment geared to the market. Buy furnishings your target families might buy and they'll have greater appreci-ation of the home.

Your goal, after all, is not a furni-ture store "showroom". It's a warm, inviting environment, within the finan-cial means of the family, that tells your target buyer he could move right in, right now, without spending a bundle on new furniture.

You'll know you've achieved this successfully when your model looks homey and feels "complete." There will be no holes. Nothing missing. And no single object will have required the bulk of the budget.

Everything looks right. And your prospects couldn't agree more!

Here's one way to communicate the lifestyle that goes along with a natural theme such as riding trails. All you need are accessories that tell the story.

18

Little Things Mean A Lot. In your total merchandising scheme, attention to detail can mean a lot in boosting sales appeal. By that I mean details or specifics in your targeted buyers' life-style.

Even though a builder may have very similar projects in different parts of the country, for example, regional differences may dictate some varied approaches to the merchandising plan in each location.

You might romance a Southern California family most effectively with a casual approach to living: lots of wicker; patios merchandised as a place to sit back and enjoy the sun; informal living areas and wide-open spaces.

The Midwest family, on the other hand, might be better wooed with traditional values such as formal living and dining areas; in effect, a home merchandized as a place for family gatherings. If weather is a factor, merchandise rooms for indoor activities through long, hard winters.

I like to visit local communities for clues to regional lifestyles. It often provides a multitude of marketing and merchandising ideas that people will identify with when they come in a home. And it helps you implement special touches that make it look as if someone cares and wants to make people feel good. For example:

• On the East Coast, buyers love touches of Americana. In Pennsylvania, an Amish quilt might win hearts in a cozy living room.

• Seashell collections in coastal regions or Indian artifacts in the Southwest will appeal to local interests and say that you are tuned into the lifestyle here.

• The ambience of a ski chalet might sell buyers in the midwest or northeast.

Tuning into regional preferences may seem time-consuming. But it will help you demonstrate to your prospects that you understand their needs and have designed homes to cater to those needs.

It can also help you avoid costly mistakes. While West Coast buyers love rough-sawn woods and light panelings, for example, East Coast buyers generally favor darker, smoother woods. They consider the rough textures "unfinished" and inappropriate for their traditional-styled homes. A little research and investigation can help you uncover regional preferences like these in time to make good impressions and avoid costly "slip-ups."

The key to merchandising models in all of the 50 states really, is to remember that the difference between decorating and merchandising is selling lifestyles suited to your location.

Sell Those Extra Bedrooms. Merchandising to market lifestyles takes in every room of the house. Even that final extra bedroom.

Secondary bedrooms, often relegated to the end of an interior designer's list of priorities, can be one of a builder's major merchandising pluses when merchandising family lifestyles in homes.

Consider, for example, that statistics indicate more than half of families buying homes now use one bedroom for a purpose other than sleeping.

You can put this fact to merchandising benefit by creating sewing rooms, play rooms, exercise, reading rooms and guest rooms that suggest the multi-use potential of these valuable "bonus" spaces. The bonus rooms you offer can motivate people to buy your homes. They may be the special "difference" that sets your home apart from the competition.

And don't forget the man of the house. There is a growing appreciation for model homes that take the male member of the buying team into special consideration. An extra bedroom designed as office or den, merchandised as his own retreat, is a good selling point. (You'll hear more about the importance of selling to the "man of the house" later).

Make the Most of Your Theme. One final point about "lifestyle" merchandising is: Think in terms of themes. If you decide to build your development around a theme, you can target that theme to appeal directly to the identified market and reap uncountable benefits.

First, you must research your market to the extent you know without a doubt the lifestyle "stories" with which it identifies. And then create a theme to tell those stories.

The kinds of themes I'm talking about may be based on a natural element—there's one for every project: a lake, citrus grove, stand of timber, knolls, rivers or the ocean.,

These "naturals" suggest instant themes and often define the type of architecture you will choose—and the lifestyle that you will build.

Golf courses, tennis courts, equestrian trails and boating marinas—the recreational facilities you plan to provide—also are good sources of theme inspiration.

You can reinforce the lifestyles these facilities provide with little reminders throughout your models—things such as tennis racquets and golf clubs, boating and riding gear and related pictures or accessories.

The overall result will be an environment that compliments the kinds of dream lifestyles your target seeks.

There's little question that builders who follow the first commandment of merchandising: Know Thy Market will be successful. The results of market research; family profiling; attention to regional differences and small details; merchandising secondary bedrooms and well-executed themes will be this: Model homes that encourage buyers to act now and buy your product.

3

The Psychology of Color.

Color can excite, surprise, soothe, refresh and stimulate. It has emotional clout and sales clout, depending on how you use it and how well you know your market's color preferences.

I have always been fascinated by color's ability to "talk" to create or alter a situation, to fire up emotions and to sell.

In fact, when I started my firm, <u>Color Design Art</u>, I incorporated "color" into the name in order to say it all in describing my priorities for merchandising model homes and other commercial developments.

I have always considered color the very foundation of successful, sales-generating model home merchandising.

I've used it, and watched it being used as an effective sales tool. And I've studied, research-ed and tested its effect on prospective buyers.

The results convince me that color sells homes!

Brilliant color, contrasted by white molding, gives this lively dining room sparkle and creates architectural impact.

Color Them Happy. My studies show that would-be buyers rate color right up there at the top—as one of the three most important factors contributing to the appeal of a model home or room.

Environment and architectural features are the other two factors rated as "most" important.

Interestingly, favored colors are more important to homeshoppers than furnishings, accessories, or even spaciousness of the room!

When you use "favorite" colors, prospective buyers respond positively and feel happy in your models. But use the wrong colors and they tend to find fault. They criticize room space or window size, for example, and walk away unhappy and unimpressed.

This underscores our need to be tuned into color trends, because when we are, we can merchandise "favorites" that create immediate, positive response.

Some Brilliant Discoveries. I find that various market categories react differently to color and often have different "favorites".

Generally, the lower-end markets are less color sensitive. As you go up the market price ladder, people become more color conscious and have more definite ideas about color.

Here's a look at three major market groups I have studied carefully, and how they responded to color:

THE CONDOMINIUM CROWD—basically composed of singles and childless couples, seems to be the least sensitive of all to color. More important to this group are such factors as architectural and designer features.

YOUNG MARRIEDS—show definite color sensitivity. They favor blue and brown, but also highly favor variations of red, green and yellow. They like color! This may, in part, be due to the fact that color is a means of self expression, and first-time buyers often are eager to express themselves, and "show-off" their new homes.

THE MADE-ITS—are most color-oriented of all. They show strong preferences for beige in home interiors, but like yellow and green followed by brown and blue. The made-its do not hedge when reacting to favorite colors, or in letting you know when they do not like the colors used!

As model merchandisers it's our job to help low-end markets and the less color sensitive groups realize the colors they like, and to provide high-end, particular markets with the colors they want and expect to see.

One way to do this is to keep abreast of color cycles. I've found that color moves in cycles which pretty much follow economic cycles. The typical cycle goes like this:

· Strong, rich colors are favored when the economy is climbing high.

· These are followed by softer pastels as the peak tapers off.

· The muted neutrals take over as the economy stabilizes and regroups.

I've found this economic-color link particularly important when dealing with first-time home buyers. When the economy is sound, they respond well to bold, bright colors which seem to hold promise of a bright future.

However, when the economy is less stable and would-be buyers are not as secure about their financial abilities, subdued and more conservative colors put them at ease.

Of course there are other outside factors influencing color trends. Fashion and furniture styles, for instance. And the color preferences we carry, or perhaps change, throughout our lives.

The cyclical nature of color, however, is always with us and suggests that we need to think ahead in terms of color shifts in sales-oriented merchandising.

Tuning into tomorrow's colors today will put you in touch with the best colors for a development that's on the line for tomorrow's markets.

The Safe and 'Never' Colors. Color, literally, is in the eye of the beholder. Whatever your buyer market category what those home-shoppers see will depend on how each eye takes in the colors of the spectrum.

And the choices they designate as "favorites" may not necessarily be they choose to be surrounded by everyday in their home interiors. The colors we choose for cars and clothes may be quite different from those we favor for our living spaces.

There are some colors, however, that appear to be universal favorites for model homes.

I call them the "never-miss" or SAFE colors. And there's good news here, because they can assure you a popular model home color scheme in every complex that will elicit happy feelings in nearly everyone. They are:

BROWN AND WARM EARTHY BROWN TONES

Everyone likes them and nobody really dislikes them! This might be, in part, due to their "neutral" appeal, or to the conditioning of wide use in clothes, furnishings, cars and building materials and so forth. They are nonirritating colors and are easy to work within decorating schemes.

WHITE AND BEIGE

They are also "safe" colors. A little "plain vanilla" maybe, but easy to decorate around and comfortable to live with. Practicality, however, demands discernment with these colors. While they may be perfect for retired or childless couples, they obviously could be poor choices in homes marketed for young families with small children and pets.

There are also some NEVER colors I suggest avoiding in model interiors at all costs. They are:

VIOLET, BLACK AND PINK

While many people like to drive or dress in violet and black, they definitely do not want to be surrounded by these colors in their homes. Almost everyone dislikes pinks as well, except as an occasional accent color or in a very feminine girl's room only. Don't build model merchandising plans around any of them!

How do you say, blue? Let me count the ways... In carpet, a country quilt, a splash of paint or bright fabrics. Say it warmly with camel, rust and beige, or cool it with reflective mirrors.

Various shades of green say different things to different markets.

Green can be cool and fresh as a fern grotto or bright and snappy as a peppermint stick...

Think in terms of WHO your prospects are before you decide WHEN, WHERE and HOW to use it.

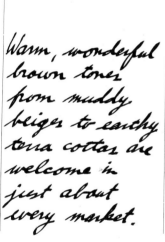

Warm, wonderful brown tones from muddy beiges to earthy terra cottas are welcome in just about every market.

Use these "mother earth" favorites to please almost everyone!

Red is racy!

But in toned down wines and russets, it's also warm and embracing.

Use red for drama or accent; but first: KNOW THY MARKET!

Beware The 'Polar' Colors: Blue, Red and Green. Blue, Red and Green, in that order, have been rated in national research as America's first favorite colors.

But I offer a word of caution about them.

I have termed them the "Polar Colors" because, surprisingly, prospective homebuyers have a definite polarized reaction to these three basic, primary colors. They either like them very much or strongly dislike them!

My advice for the Polar Colors is this: Use them with care because there is no middle ground. When you decorate a model in a complex with a Polar Color, counter-balance with another model in a "safe" color.

The intense acceptance/denial pattern for these polar colors gives pause for some psychological theorizing or Monday morning quarterbacking:

Why do folks have a love/hate relationship with Polar Colors? I think it's a matter of degree and how you use them. Muted, darkened or dusty tones can convert non-believers into lovers!

I believe the ardent "anti" attitudes are shaped much by the tone, hue and intensity as well as quality of the color used.

Red, particularly, is an emotionally potent color. Simply "seeing red" can speed up the pulse rate, raise the blood pressure and increase the rate of respiration.

Some people like the warm, stimulating nature of red, while others feel aggravated by it. However, when red becomes a warm russet, home shoppers often find it less "aggressive" and more "dramatic", "exciting", "comfortable" and "cozy". Positive reactions.

Blue generally is identified as a "cool" color, but in warmed-up, revved up tones it can become "relaxing" or "serene" and even "cozy" when combined, say, with warm carmels or creams and beiges.

And green, in carefully selected hues, is often identified as "cool", "clean", and "refreshing". These kinds of descriptions echo the kinds of emotional responses builders say sell houses.

Importantly, the color "moods" you create, and the resulting buyer responses, will vary with the tone, hue, intensity and quantity of color used, and the combinations of colors you select for your model interiors.

This doesn't mean you should be timid with color. It means you should be selective and do your marketing research.

The careful—and often bold—use of color can provide the excitement and stimuli that turns on buyers and sales.

And the positive thing about it is that color need not add much to your merchandising costs.

4

Putting Color To Work.

Color talks. It communicates. We say as much in our language: When we're sad, "we're blue." When we're angry, "we see red." When we're jealous, "we're green with envy."

Your goal in choosing model home colors should be to create a color-schemed environment that speaks <u>your buyer's language.</u> That is, it should be stimulating but also cozy, warm, loving, comfortable and inviting on his terms. If you achieve this—and you can with the right colors—then your models are talking!

Choice of specific colors can communicate sales-generating messages that turn on buyer emotions. There are three guidelines to remember in selecting model colors that work for sales success. They must be geared to:

- market trends;
- buyer preferences;
- and just as important,

to enhancing the interior features of the home, not over-shadowing them!

Blue may be HER favoite color, but mixed with warm, pine-finished woods and plaids, it speaks a man's language, too.

A Lesson in Color Technique. This latter point (enhance, don't overwhelm) came home to me dramatically in a project I did in Southern California during our early years in this business. It was a turning point for me and my staff because it made it very clear to us that there is a major difference between "decorating" with color and "merchandising" with color.

We created an interior design that was a phenomenal color statement. We used very bold magentas and oranges combined with lots of mirror which intensified the color scheme and literally shouted for attention.

Well, it certainly drew attention! Crowds thronged to see the model home, or, I should say, the interior design job.

Unfortunately, they were so overwhelmed by the decor they really retained no concept of floorplan or home features when they left. The color was too dazzling, too much.

While crowds continued to pour in to see the "show" no one was buying that particular model. Happily, however, we turned around the situation by making some strategic changes.

We took out the bright orange tile in the entry and toned down interior color by white-washing wood paneling for a softened effect. We also eliminated a brilliant "show-stopper" accessory—a graphic in orange and magenta.

The end result was that sales picked up when we softened our approach. Probably only one in a hundred home buyers would have selected that energetic color combination for his own home.

Sometimes color is most effective when it speaks softly...

This is not to say that you cannot take a creative approach to color. My point is, you must be tuned into your market.

The market for this particular project actually was a down-home "family" market that wanted cozy, home-style interiors rather than the young market around which we had built our bold color scheme. I learned an invaluable lesson as a result: Good color merchandising is never an accident!

And it's not a designer's ego trip either. It's doing your homework—researching market preferences. And it's coloring and decorating models to appeal directly to those preferences and enhancing homes in an honest way to make the most of good features.

Create Color Continuity. Once you've done your homework and determined your market's color tastes, I suggest you choose a color scheme for each model and carry it throughout every room. (If there are several models in a complex, then choose a different color scheme for each model.)

This continuity of color within each house will:
· Create immediate visual impact.
· Help your models "flow" well.
· Create a memorable identify for each model in a complex.

Home shoppers later will recall their favorites as the "Burgundy model", the "Yellow one", etc.

There are important color rules to remember concerning the size of houses. In condominiums and small homes, stay with light colors to maximize space. White, beige, pale gray or soft pastels, for example, are "expansive" colors that will open up small rooms. In a large house, your options become more versatile. You can be more daring. You can use bold, deep colors to emphasize a space and you'll have more leverage for creating special visual effects with color.

The Color Trilogy. A good way to build model home color schemes is to select three basic colors. This trilogy of colors will provide you an easy and basic plan to work with. The three should include:

· PRIMARY COLOR—usually the color for carpet and large furniture upholstery

· ACCENT COLOR—for smaller upholstered pieces of furniture such as dining room chairs, and for pillows, trims, parts of bedspreads, etc.

· SURPRISE COLOR—a tingling accent to spice up your color theme. You'll use this color in accessories.

Here are some examples of model home color schemes that I've seen used successfully:

PRIMARY COLOR: Beige
ACCENT COLOR: Burgundy
SUPRISE COLOR: Emerald Green

PRIMARY COLOR: Rust
ACCENT COLOR: Beige
SURPRISE COLOR: Navy Blue

PRIMARY COLOR: Blue
ACCENT COLOR: White
SURPRISE COLOR: Yellow

An important guideline to remember for a complex with several models is to choose color schemes from model to model in visually-appealing order. You won't want to have all the light colors, say, or all the "polar colors" bunched up together. You'll want to intersperse the brightly colored plans with some softer, more subdued ones, etc.

Also, make sure your last model sings! The finale should be happy and uplifting to give buyers the feeling that "all's well that ends well."

Soft To Bold—Three Ways To Go. As you plan your color strategy, there are three approaches you might consider for overall color scheming in each home:

1. SOFT, SOOTHING—You can create a very soft, quiet and soothing background that is neutral—a beige or soft pastel, for example—then bring out color in bright accents that give your room an exclamation point for interest.

2. BOLD—You may decide to create a lot of visual excitement with color in large doses. To do this, put your strongest color in the carpet and in the fabrics for large furniture. Then tone everything else down in the background.

3. MONOCHROMATIC—Another, very different approach, the idea here is to keep everything in one basic hue, using softer and bolder tones of the main color to accent the overall effect.

Whichever of the three plans you choose, an initial decision on your color approach is your first, most basic task. This will dictate your carpet color. All else will follow in place, according to the plan. Remember, carpet color will be the largest single amount of color you use in the model home.

44

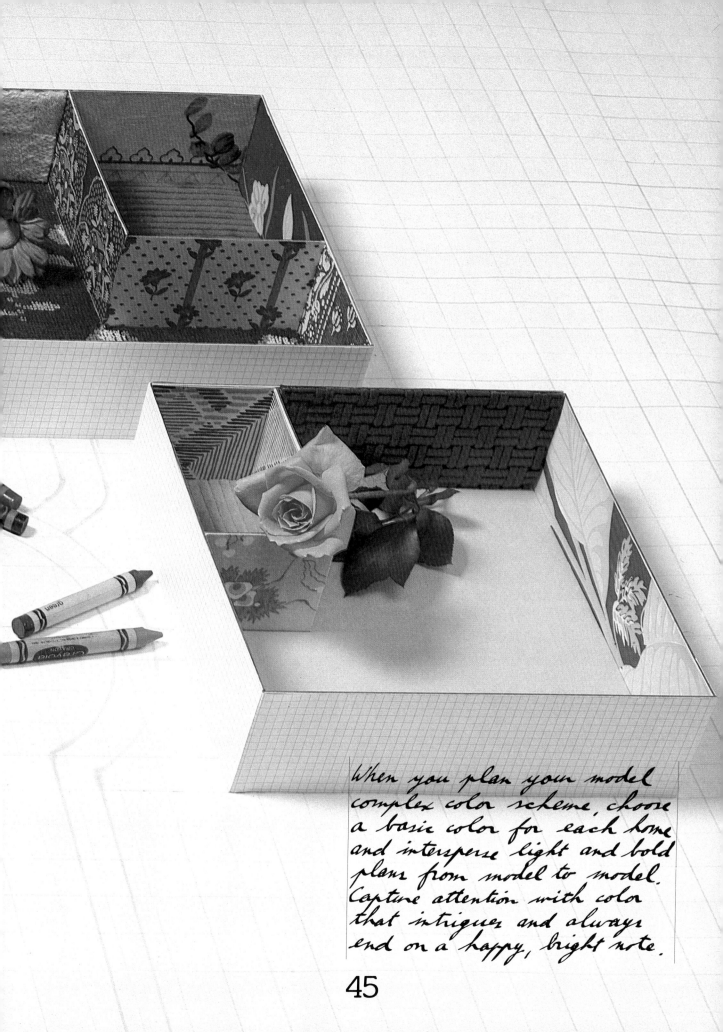

When you plan your model
complex color scheme, choose
a basic color for each home
and intersperse light and bold
plans from model to model.
Capture attention with color
that intrigues and always
end on a happy, bright note.

45

Coordinate With Furniture. I believe the most inspiring interiors are those in which color, style of furnishings and architecture ALL work together to create a memorable experience.

This can and does happen when we train our eyes to recognize workable combinations, and put our design skills to work to create outstanding effects, not mere mediocrity.

It doesn't necessarily cost more. It simply requires the right attitude—a determination to seek out the best for your project. I recommend you take note of merchandisers who do this well and follow their lead. Take note of how they color key interiors to wood tones, surface materials such as brick or tile, and to furniture style.

I have found that certain colors work best with specific furniture styles, and I key colors to those styles when I use them in this way:

· The "Country" look—warm, brown and earth tones are best for this informal kind of charm.

· Country French—pale, subdued colors are perfect accents.

· English Tudor—deeper, richer tones such as burgundies, deep blues or forest green give authenticity here.

· Indoor/Outdoor or "Garden" look—bright cheerful, garden colors and green and yellow bring this look alive. Use fushia and tulip tones for accent.

· Traditional—neutral colors and naturals; beige and carmel are good.

· Oriental—spots of bright color such as lacquer red, black or orange are essential.

East meets West in this interplay of classic white and lacquer black.

46

Color Them Comfortable. When architecture is very basic, in low-end price markets most particularly, you'll be better off using basic colors. These will usually work best with the architectural situation and will probably make your audience in this market most comfortable.

Good "basic" combinations might be:
- Beige, brown and a pale blue
- or a combination of all naturals: carmels, beiges and earth tones

In low price markets or with very basic architectural plans it's usually best to avoid unusual, extraordinary "fashion" colors.

These should be reserved for high-end developments with a more sophisticated market. In higher price ranges buyers are more likely to seek the rich visual interest of extraordinary colors that intrigue the imagination, show sensitivity to trends and express personal style.

In many instances, unusual "fashion" colors can help highlight distinctive architectural designs in a more interesting way than basic colors. But, keep in mind that "fashion" colors are often available only in expensive "designer" fabrics and accessories. Upper-end markets will be better able to afford them, but you want to keep your budget in mind before you plan a color scheme around them.

Accessories generally are plentiful and easily found in basic colors. Once manufacturers know that a color has caught on they use it in profusion.

Monochromatic color warms this room and highlights a pitched ceiling.

Kitchen, Bath: Color Them Bright.

Special attention to color is needed in two of the most important spaces in every model home—kitchens and bathrooms. You can color them both bright for best results.

Since both kitchen and bath are smaller than the major living areas, they can afford the impact of more color—first, for effect and as a "selling" tool; second, because we spend less time in these rooms, so stronger color will not overwhelm or become tiresome.

The woman of the house, particularly, should be excited when she comes into that kitchen. Color can help generate the excitement, enthusiasm and good feelings that tell her she'd be "happy" here.

Color sparks up bathrooms with personality, and makes them seem larger than actual square footage. Stay within the basic color scheme you've chosen for your model, but go bolder and brighter for bigger impact.

Remember that color does not apply to paint only. You can add color with wallpaper, wood paneling and accessories as well. And pay attention to lighting. Use it to make the most of your color touches and to accent color spots.

Capitalize On Color. In the final analysis, color is one of the most important ingredients in your merchandising mix of life-giving, personalizing and accent strategies.

It can pull the eye to the design features you want to emphasize. It can also de-emphasize problem areas. It can cozy up wide open spaces or wake up small ones. It's not a cure-all but it certainly can dress up your best points and de-emphasize those you'd like to downplay. When you need to create an illusion of space—either less or more—keep in mind the following two basic rules of color:

· Cool blues and green make an area recede. These colors tend to "back off."

· On the other hand, the warm reds and oranges "advance." These visually embracing colors can lessen apparent space or lower ceiling height, for example.

To maximize merchandising effectiveness, a builder can never go wrong by learning and understanding all the psychological and visual effects color can and does have on the home-buying public. Learn to experiment with color. But more important, learn to use it for optimum effect by paying close attention to economic and social trends that apply to and will effect prospects and their color-related buying moods in your market.

Space stretching color accentuates the positive in this small kitchen and lifts the spirits.

51

5

Architecture: If You've Got It, Flaunt It!

We've talked about merchandising as the wrapping on the model home package, the frosting on the cake.

But now, let's get down to the cake itself—the architecture and special architectural features.

Research shows that prospective buyers consider architectural features THE most important selling points in model homes.

Cathedral ceilings and stained glass windows, bold archways, level variations, window seats, sunken bathtubs, spiraling staircases, wood beams, et. al. These are the pluses that add interest, personality and custom touches to your homes, so <u>merchandise them to immediately capture the eye!</u>

Whatever the price range of your models, architectural points of interest tell your target buyer that he's getting something extra, something special for his money.

Here's a first impression that's memorable! Border carpet in soft color helps emphasize the drama and immediate impact.

Accentuate the Positive. While many architectural features certainly speak well for themselves, savvy merchandising will make sure they speak directly to your market.

For example:

· If you've gone to the expense of building a two-story fireplace in the living room, wrap it up with brick and/or wood to make it an eye-catching focal point. Excitement and glamour in seemingly small details such as this can make a big impact on how a buyer perceives special features in your models in contrast to other homes.

· Create convenient conversation areas near fireplaces to emphasize these selling points and to kindle good spirits and sales. This will have particular appeal to couples who entertain a lot and to older couples.

· Play on the interest of level variations from room to room with a change of carpet or wall-covering. If spaces are small, do the reverse—expand them with a continuous "flow" of carpet and wall color. Young "moderns", in particular, in both condominium and detached home markets, are impressed with contemporary architectural design features highlighted this way.

· Use mirrors, mantles, shelving, wood panels, chair railing and molding to emphasize high ceilings and high-reaching walls, and to create focal points on wide-open spaces. The resulting expansiveness appeals to almost everyone.

· Play up space-expanding vistas and customized windows with window treatment that enhances, not overwhelms the view. On the other hand, when windows are misplaced, "corrective" window treatment merchandising can be used to play them down or to overcome their architectural shortcomings. Few people appreciate small windows unless they have a decorative purpose. Big is always best in windows!

· Bring the outdoors in, and expand living space whenever possible, by "extending" rooms into atriums and patios visually, with continuing floor treatment and colors, glass doors and wide open windows. This open-space merchandising always wins hearts in warm climates where outdoor living is an important fact of life.

Wood ties the varied architectural elements here together in a warm and pleasing package.

Without wood's
unifying effect
the room might
have appeared
"chopped up".

Innerspace: Quality vs. Quantity. Room size and shape are the most important architectural features in any and every home according to buyer surveys conducted by my firm. But the way space is perceived by buyers may have little to do with actual square footage and much to do with merchandising.

As a point of example, during one research project we conducted, prospects toured two identical family rooms. One featured a space-expanding mirrored bookcase along a side wall. In homeshoppers' minds, this room was perceived as larger and more spacious than the identical room without the treatment.

They saw it as bigger and better because the family room was "opened up" with the mirrors and built-in book-shelves. They helped reduce furniture clutter and expand on room size. Home-shoppers made it very clear they liked the results of these additions. Big was better and more appealing.

There are other ways to make prospective buyers think BIG:

· Use light colors.

· Take advantage of space-expanding views.

· Keep furniture light and trim.

· Use the same carpeting throughout the model home to avoid a chopped-up appearance and provide visual flow.

If you're dealing with expansive, wide-open rooms, you may want to go the other way and give the room cozy warmth. Soaring 18-ft. ceilings are high on most buyers' lists of architectural pluses, but they sometimes can mean too much of a good thing.

This monochromatic color scheme has two-fold purpose. It emphasizes the architecture and visually enlarges the scope of the room.

Light colours make the most of a bedroom retreat. Notice how the double door and fireplace help expand the space.

Arched bookshelves are a merchandising addition here to help further accentuate Spanish architectural elements already existing -- brick fireplace, terra cotta tiles, heavy beams and double doors.

Understated elegance is reflected in this ceiling, mirrored to highlight the intrigue of level variations.

Here's a conversation pit big enough for a cocktail party, but fireplace treatment and accessories keep it cozy.

A vast amount of space may in fact seem cold, empty, even frightening to a prospective buyer who has to "fill it up." He may decide he can't afford the cost of furnishing.

In large spaces the merchandising job is to warm up the room and reduce it to more human proportions without suggesting the need for expensive furniture. Here are some ideas that work:

· Different textures can break up space and make it more interesting. Wood, brick, cork, wallpaper, tile and fabrics on walls and ceilings bring large spaces into cozy proportion.

· A coat of light beige or natural paint can warm up high volume walls without interfering with the architectural statement. A natural wallpaper, for instance a grasscloth, will create the same effect and provide the added dimension of texture.

· Wood is a natural for warming up space. In high volume areas I like to wrap both ceilings and walls with wood.

· Bold patterns in wallpaper, and wall molding to define space and frame furniture, also both help cut a room down to comfortable size without eliminating valuable spaciousness.

Market Kitchen and Bath Features. People always seem to gather in the kitchen of the homes they visit, and model home visitors are no exception to this rule.

The kitchen and bathrooms, after-all, are important decision-making areas in the home-buying process. These are two rooms in which you will want to take extra care to merchandise architectural features. Accessories are always good eye-openers that help draw attention to special features easily and inexpensively.

In the kitchen, draw the eye to a pass-through by piling it with picnic fare. Merchandise a butcher block island with the latest gourmet cookware, and an inviting breakfast nook with built-in booths and an overhead skylight that lets in the sunshine. Call attention to a menu-planning desk with appropriate seating, cookbooks and a calculator. Prospects will love the atmosphere and the architectural delights they discover.

That bathroom atrium should look as lush as the Garden of Eden. So fill it with plenty of plants. Double the impact—and size—of a sunken master tub with mirrors, and add the pizzazz of more green plants all around to establish a spa-like corner retreat.

If your bathrooms need a boost in the architectural department, add floor to ceiling shelves stocked with plush towels and scented lotions and potions. A built-in magazine rack could hold up-to-date reading material.

The possibilities are endless. You can have fun making these important areas first class showrooms with extra attention to architectural detail.

Plan Ahead. The time to think about architectural merchandising is at the very beginning of your development plan, at that point when you hire your architect and first discuss floorplans. This is also the time to commit yourself to the best you can afford.

No doubt, a two-story brick fireplace costs more than a coat of paint. A wood-paneled wall more than a plain wall, and French doors or bay windows, more than sliding glass doors.

However, the most successful builders I know have learned that extra investment in architectural extras suited to the individual home will pay off later in merchandising success.

Today's buyers expect more for their money—more comfort, style and creative design. And they will buy from the builder who exhibits good taste, and makes a point of going that extra step to provide a quality product.

Consulting ahead of time with interior merchandising experts can help you plan special features in the right places—before interior design is implemented.

This kind of forward-thinking can prove invaluable in merchandising, and save dollars in costly slip-ups later. I've seen many cases in which a simple rearrangement of cabinetry, doors, windows, built-in features and windows could have improved a model interior a thousand-fold. Even a matter so simple as moving a window slightly left or right can have important visual impact.

The best rule of thumb is: when in doubt, consult an interior merchandising professional. Seek advice on placement and treatment of architectural pluses and you'll undoubtedly have superb results.

In addition, the interior design process will be supplanted by a solid architectural foundation geared for merchandising impact.

6

Build Up Sales With Built-Ins.

It's no secret that architectural amenities sell homes. If you've built them into homes in your development you're a step ahead of the competition already.

However, if your development plans have not afforded as many architectural points of interest as you'd like— or you feel are needed to attract your market—then add them on later. Use built-ins.

It's impossible to over-emphasize the sales-generating qualities of built-ins such as party-inspiring wet bars, space-saving book-shelves, handy room dividers, planters or decorative add-ons such as paneling, trim, wainscotting and chair railings.

These are not only utilitarian and attractive features, they are delightfully unex-pected surprises that excite home shoppers and turn them on to the potential of your model floorplans. They make immediate first impressions and memorable lasting ones.

What male could resist the fanta-sies offered in this futuristic stainless-steel-wrapped batche-lor's pad? Eat your heart out, James Bond!

Built-Ins Have Sales Appeal. Because I have always believed in the sales-inducing qualities of built-ins, I conducted professional research to give factual, sound basis to what I've always intuitively "felt" was true. That is, that built-ins have sales-appeal.

The research (and several hundred surveyed homebuyers) confirmed my belief that <u>rooms with built-ins generate more positive buyer reaction than rooms without them.</u>

The research was conducted at two separate California developments with identical floor plans. Its purpose was to determine the impact of identical rooms with and without built-ins on prospective buyers.

Very simply, the findings told me that built-ins can help build up sales in three important ways:

1. Built-ins are one of the four most important factors in overall room appeal in model homes.

Size is the single most important factor in room appeal; buyers expect a certain amount of space. They expect convenient room shapes. They have definite ideas about color and they say built-ins are the next most important factor contributing to a room's appeal!

I believe this is because built-ins illustrate how prospective buyers can personalize a room and also make it efficient. Built-ins are specifically designed to compliment the space in a room, whereas furniture cannot be as specifically adapted to a room's design.

A rating as fourth most important factor in rooms and their appeal to prospects is something no builder should overlook in his merchandising program. In short, built-ins are key sales tools. I suggest using them in every room of the home.

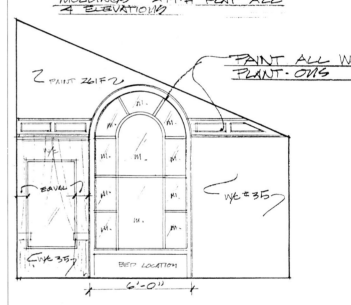

Complete, detailed drawings are imperative for superbly-executed built-ins. Buyers like the custom quality of a glamorous headboard or functional shelving.

2. They are extremely effective for directing appeal to a specific target market.

Nothing will sell a home faster to a gourmet cook than a kitchen island loaded with gourmet gadgets. Families with school-aged children are attracted by built-in bookshelves. Mothers with young children love handy shelves and storage bins for stashing toys away quickly and easily. In fact, there are few people who don't appreciate the space-saving, convenience and beauty of built-ins.

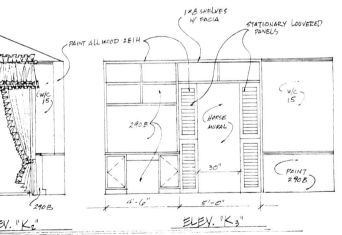

More specifically, however, buyers surveyed identified some built-ins with certain kinds of people. They associated bookshelves with older, sophisticated families with older children. They perceived homes with wet bars, shelves for collectibles and bookcases as homes of families who stay home a lot and entertain frequently. These survey results tell me that you can key your homes to some very specific buyers by the built-ins you use. And you can create status in homes by using built-ins. Buyers, for the most part, associated built-ins with higher-end developments. You can use these results effectively by using built-ins to upgrade lower-end projects in prospects' minds. And to maximize the exclusivity and luxury of higher-end custom homes.

3. Buyers are highly likely to add built-ins as optional features to their own newly-purchased homes.

Only the handiest of buyers may get around to building them by himself. But offer built-ins to your buyers at a reasonable price and most will pay you for this option. They appreciate the idea of built-in interior design features that are customized to the home, be they built-in bookshelves, headboards for beds or planter boxes in a kitchen. Most perceive these as luxury, customized additions. So make them available! And if you can't provide the actual built-ins, provide the plans. Your buyers will appreciate this gesture to help them improve their own new homes.

Research results additionally reinforce my belief that built-ins add luxury, warmth, coziness and personality to homes, and make rooms seem larger, better organized and more "customized."

What You See Is Indeed What You Get.
There are some important considerations
to keep in mind when planning built-in
merchandising strategy. Most important
is the fact that today's buyers are a
sophisticated group who expect the
most for their money and want to
know exactly what they will get for
their dollars.

So make it perfectly clear. Tell
shoppers if the built-ins are not included
in the basic price of the home, but make
them available as optional features at
reasonable cost. Or make the plans for
the built-ins available. You may want to
do it this way for best results: Prepare a
fun "announcement" card to display on
the built-ins saying that you have plans
for them, telling buyers how and where
to purchase them. Then use a headline
like: "We have plans for you!" Most
buyers will appreciate the builder who
goes that extra step.

a bedroom yes. But a study area
and hobby room too. A cache
of built-ins turn an ordinary
bedroom into a teenage boy's
private retreat.

Which Built-Ins To Build In? If there is a clear favorite built-in among potential buyers it is bookcases. They are seen as a symbol of a well-educated family, as space savers, as a good way to achieve a "decorator" look in a room. You can't go wrong when you include them in important rooms.

Wet bars are another universal favorite.

Shelves, especially when dressed up with fret work; entertainment centers; special headboard treatment in bedrooms; lattice work, and storage cabinets—particularly in dens and secondary bedrooms—are other built-ins that prospective buyers seem to appreciate and ask for most often.

Chair railings and moldings shaped into wall panels, mantels over fireplaces, and stained glass window insets, because of the decorative and personalizing touches they add to rooms, are others in top demand.

Interestingly, the living room and the family room are the rooms homebuyers consider the most important locations for built-ins. Here they see them as adding function and dimension to rooms. On the other hand, most perceive a built-in in bedrooms as more of a luxury item than a functional one

This information can help you determine where to put dollars into built-in extras in your own models. If the home is in a low-to-middle priced development, concentrate built-ins in living areas, but add them to bedrooms when you need to perk up ordinary surroundings. In higher-priced projects built-ins can be included with a free hand to illustrate a home's custom quality or potential.

Bookcases are always a favorite!

71

The floorplans are identical, but a slip of fretwork turns one room into a romantic update of a bygone era.

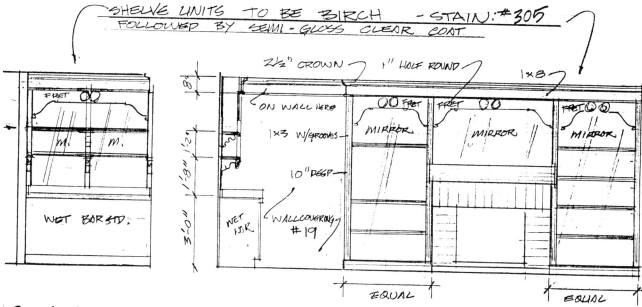

SHELVE UNITS TO BE BIRCH - STAIN: #305
FOLLOWED BY SEMI-GLOSS CLEAR COAT

FRET
M.   M.
WET BOR STD.

2½" CROWN   1" HALF ROUND   1×8
ON WALL HERE
1×3 W/GROOVES
FRET   FRET
MIRROR   MIRROR   MIRROR
10" DEEP
WET FIR
WALLCOVERING #19
8"   1'-8"   1'-2"   3'-0"
EQUAL   EQUAL

Sq. footage is the same, but buyers see the room with built-ins, below, as larger!

Fretwork and shelving backed by mirror give expanded dimension.

Keep These In Mind. Here's a list of possibilities you can apply to your own built-in considerations. There's a place in almost every room for these special touches. In each development, take a good look at the market and you're likely to come up with many of your own ideas.

> Bookcases, both open and closed
> Paneling, trim and molding on walls everywhere
> Stained glass insets
> Mirrors
> Closet drawers and cubicles
> Shoe racks
> Fireplace mantels
> Window seats
> Log bins
> Decorative beams
> Planters
> Spice racks
> Wine/stemware racks
> Custom towel racks
> Hampers
> Magazine racks
> Desks, study and organizational areas
> Home entertainment centers
> Pegboards
> Shelves of any sort
> Work benches
> Storage bins
> Snack counters
> Molding

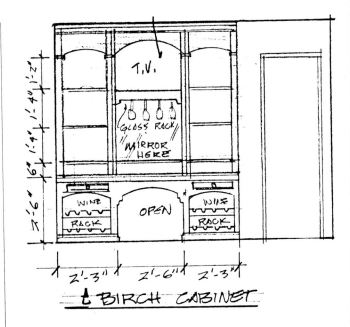

$\mathcal{L}$ BIRCH CABINET

Innovative built-ins improve a room's storage and style.

While the possibilities are overwhelming, they do not have to overwhelm your budget. All it takes is creative merchandising to sell built-ins, and again, a thorough knowledge of your market. Every item you use—from every pillow, plant and drop of paint to every built-in—should be designed to involve the prospective buyer in that home.

The more someone feels at home, the more likely he or she will want to buy and live there. That's why a good merchandising plan can implement as many built-in options as possible.

With this kind of "built-in" service, you'll be building a lot more than bookcases. Even more than sales. You'll be building a reputation for quality and caring that will be selling your homes now and for years to come. And, I'll give you a built-in guarantee on that!

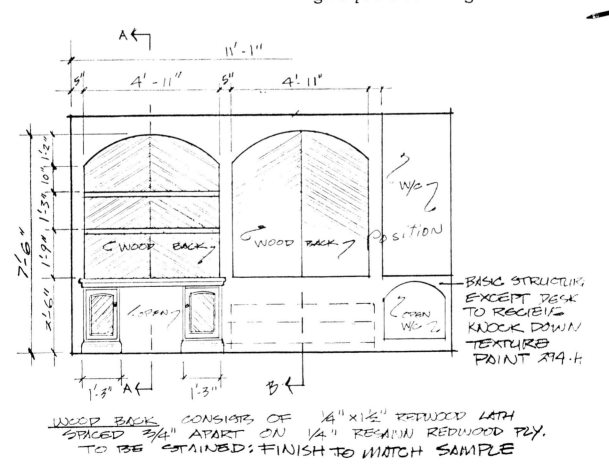

WOOD BACK CONSISTS OF 1/4" X 1 1/2" REDWOOD LATH SPACED 3/4" APART ON 1/4" RESAWN REDWOOD PLY. TO BE STAINED: FINISH TO MATCH SAMPLE

7

The Nuts And Bolts

Floor Coverings
Wall Coverings
Window Treatments
Furniture
Lighting & Fixtures
Counter Tops

These are the basics. The "Nuts and Bolts" of good model home merchandising.

Floor, wall and window treatments are the "wrappings" I mentioned in chapter one that tie up your models in appealing merchandising packages.

Furniture, lighting, counter tops and fixtures are important mood makers that will help put your prospects in the mood to buy.

The patterns, colors, textures and designs of all the Nuts and Bolts will have much to say about the background moods you create. For example:

· A floral print wallpaper may give your room the appropriate period feeling; a mylar, the right contemporary dash.

Bathrooms are the showcase rooms, more exciting than ever with use of colorful surface materials.

· Light-colored carpet can set the appropriate background for a "sunny" garden look, while rich wood floors might support an English or provincial theme.

· Choice of furniture style can also determine moods and direct appeal to various sub-groups within your target market. One model decked out in contemporary furnishings may attract a younger market, and a second model, furnished in traditional styles, the older buyer.

As you will see, the Nuts and Bolts necessarily must come together in a well-executed merchandising plan to tie up a total image with which your buyers can relate. Every item should be coordinated to sell that image or tell your mood story.

Various factors, including size, shape and purpose of your rooms, will have bearing on how you handle the Nuts and Bolts as far as patterns, boldness, depth and color. Keep in mind that they are intimately and undeniably linked with each other and with the overall theme of your models. They can and will make the difference between a ho-hum first impression and one that packs immediate punch.

The nuts and bolts here are daring but endearing. Plaid carpeting, a twist on usual flooring, bold shutters and built-in seating suggest koffee-klatching and family interplay would be pleasing here amidst the clamor of cooking.

Flooring: The Cover Story. Choice of floor coverings will be one of the primary and most important decisions in your total merchandising plan, because carpeting provides the largest amount of color in the model home. It will be the basis on which you'll anchor all of the other Nuts and Bolts.

There are three basic categories of flooring: Soft flooring such as rugs and carpeting; hard surface flooring, such as hardwood floors, ceramic, adobe and other types of tiles; brick, slate and flagstone, etc.; and resilient flooring such as vinyl and rubber tiles, and linoleum.

Most of the time I recommend using wall-to-wall carpeting throughout a model because of its attractiveness, easy upkeep and most important, flow of color.

Go ahead and carpet right into the kitchens and bathrooms to keep that flow continuous. Even though most people do not generally carpet these areas, from a merchandising point of view it's good business. It gives a model a well-coordinated look, prevents the chopped up appearance created by a sudden patch of vinyl or linoleum or other alternate flooring more common in these areas. Carpet also warms up the kitchen and baths. I find that vinyls, linoleums and other hard surface coverings too often tend to have a cold, institutional look that is not as sales enhancing as the wall to wall color and warmth of carpeting.

You'll find that most people understand that carpeting is not "standard" in kitchens and bathrooms. Nevertheless, it's a good idea to make this perfectly clear in signs, brochures or other sales materials. Spell out what is standard and exactly what optional alternatives are available.

There are two exceptions to my rule of thumb about carpeting models in entirety that are borne of practicality:

1. The Model Home Entry: Here tile or any other type of "hard" surface may be preferrable since this area gets more traffic and more wear than other areas.

2. Large bonus or family rooms, isolated rooms, hobby and play rooms: In these spaces you may want alternate floorings for special effect, to demonstrate easy care or practicality. If so, choose colors that coordinate and blend handsomely with the original carpeting.

One way to add color and interest to overall carpeting is to scatter throw rugs on top for special effects. Hardwood floors in some selected rooms also give a special warmth.

However, if you use hardwood floors, do so with care. They make more noise and require more maintenence than carpeting, and these are two important considerations in model home presentation and upkeep.

Even though the carpet is blue, the other nuts and bolts warm up this space and make it a family place.

Walls: Wrap Them Up. From a simple coat of paint to wood panelings and the varied textures of wallpaper and fabric, the decorating possibilities for walls seem endless. You'll want to be sure to wrap walls with color and excitement for backgrounds that support your merchandising themes and stimulate your buyers' interest. Here are some tips on how to do it:

Paint: It's a quick, easy and inexpensive way to add color to the walls.

Wood: Use it in strips, paneling, frames and molding, as a sure way to provide warmth, color and atmosphere in rooms.

Wallpaper and fabrics: On walls they have many-faceted functions. Not only do they lend color, texture and design, but prestige and personality as well, depending on pattern and material.

Once you've selected your wall covering technique, you may want to follow these hints:

· Use paint to warm up stark white walls and ceilings, especially in large, volume spaces. You needn't use bold colors. Beige and natural tones provide enough color to warm up the space without detracting from the architecture.

· Wrap wood paneling up walls and right onto ceilings. Use light wood finishes in small rooms that are color-coordinated with carpeting. Go to middle and darker wood finishes in larger spaces.

· Always coordinate wallpaper patterns with other patterns in your room—those in draperies, upholstery fabrics, countertops and flooring. Everything should blend!

· Wallpaper patterns in one room should coordinate with those visible in other rooms.

· Use medium and large prints in wallpapers for large volume areas. Small prints will get lost.

Windows: Let There Be Light! Cozy is one thing, cooped up is another. Nothing draws the curtain on sales faster than models that feel dark, stuffy or closed in. So, let there be light! That means never cover windows unless, of course, the view is so unsightly it's a deterrent to sales.

The best approach to almost any window treatment is to think of the view beyond as a picture and frame it. Your frame may be charming shutters, formal draperies and valances or country-fresh curtains, depending on theme and style. If there's a million-dollar view to be had, a real stop-in-your-tracks view, be sure to merchandise it to the utmost. Lead prospects to the window with inviting window seats or strategic furniture arrangement and a window treatment that pours forth plenty of light. Think in terms of framing the picture beyond for optimum effect.

Following are a few hints for merchandising model home windows to best advantage:

· Be budget-conscious by using "show" or "model home" draperies with side ties and valances rather than more expensive, fully-operating draperies.

· If you use shutters, use wide louvers. They're more attractive and easier to clean and maintain.

· Use Venetian blinds with caution. The very narrow blinds that have become popular in home use are attractive and come in a wide range of colors. However, a warning—they often tempt browsers to turn, adjust and lift them, only to create havoc with your merchandising efforts. You may end up with blinds that are askew, broken or maladjusted and detract from the good looks you've worked hard to achieve. If you use them in models, set them the way you want them, then remove the controls.

· Call attention to unusual windows that are out of reach—skylights and clerestory windows—with frames of wood or shelving beneath or nearby.

· To mask an outdoor eyesore (or less-than-perfect view) use a light-emitting lace drapery to cover the window. It will permit sunlight to permeate the room without calling attention to what's outside.

· If walls provide plenty of interest and you don't need window treatment, leave windows "undone". In many California projects hanging plants are often used as an alternative window treatment. The result is a feeling of airiness that makes the most of an exceptional exterior view.

Furniture: What Would Your Buyer Buy? The important thing to remember about furniture is that it is only one element of interior merchandising. It is an accessory, a single course in the meal but certainly not the entire feast.

Since the furnishings "bill of fare" you present in your model homes will be offered to a mass market, as opposed to an individual client whose tastes you would know well, you'll want the menu to be pleasing but not extreme.

The best quideline in selecting furniture—and I can't overstate it enough—is to concentrate on your market. Study the target buyer's lifestyle and income. Then buy furnishings a typical buyer might buy—items that meet both his budget and expectations. If you zero in on your market, you'll avoid wasting dollars trying to sell the buyer who is not a logical candidate.

I've learned from experience that too much money spent on furnishings, can and does frighten away some prospects. The first-time buyer assuming a mortgage for the first time, or the move-up buyer assuming a larger mortgage than before, may be intimidated by overly expensive items.

While these folks may aspire to the luxury of fine furniture, if they can't afford it now, they may decide they can't afford your house either. So, don't scare them away!

Another point to keep in mind when selecting furniture is that merchandising is the total package. You don't want prospects falling in love with a beautiful sofa or table and forgetting your floorplans. You want them to love the total effect of the home.

84

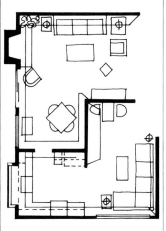

Take a close look at furniture arrangements in these two rooms and then compare with identical plans on the next page.

Vary Furniture Themes. It's usually a good idea to employ several different furniture themes in each model complex—a different style in each home will appeal to a variety of preferences within the market.

Once you've selected a theme or style, be consistent throughout the model. You won't want to begin with glass and chrome in the living room and end up with early American four-poster beds in the bedroom.

This does not mean that everything should be matched perfectly, because people certainly don't furnish their own homes that way. It's unrealistic to stock models as if everything just arrived in one shipment from the factory. The results may be as sterile as a discount furniture storeroom window, or the motel down the street where every room is a clone of the next.

The secret is to stay within a theme but add enough variation to provide interest and excitement. What's really more important than style of furniture, is the way you use it in your models.

Put a bed, dresser and chaise lounge in a bedroom to demonstrate space. Arrange desk, built-ins or special items so that secondary bedrooms become hobby rooms and dens.

In family rooms, arrange furniture to illustrate how eating space (if need be), game areas and conversation or reading areas all can be accommodated.

You want your buyers to realize they could move right in with their own belongings and without the purchase of a house-full of new furnishings.

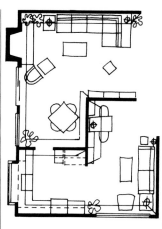

Notice in the lower photo how table, chairs and painting take the place of built-ins used in identical floorplan on preceding page. Both are saleable alternatives.

Lighting: Some Bright Ideas. Lighting can entice prospects into a room and it also may turn them away. It can be soft, mellow, meditative, sensuous, dramatic and romantic. It can be bright, snappy, glamorous and utilitarian.

It can call attention to special design or architectural features with spotlighting; it can create a wide range of moods and generate an equally wide range of emotional responses, depending on how you use it and on the light fixtures you select.

Decide on the effects you hope to achieve, then make sure your lighting and your light fixtures will produce those desired effects and contribute to the richness of your interiors.

On occasion, you may want to choose an unusual or elaborate light fixture to support a special theme when a budget affords it.

In addition to themed fixtures for special effect, you may want to consider built-in recessed lighting for living and family rooms. Fluorescent boxes and luminious ceilings are bright ideas for perking up kitchens. And track lighting or spotlighting techniques can be used to mark areas for special use, or to highlight design and architectural features—a picture grouping on a brick wall, a built-in display cabinet, a stained glass widow, a game table or game area, or a work center, for example.

Lighting and light fixtures should serve a dual role in your merchandising plan:

1. They should provide quality and quantity illumination to highlight special features in your models.

2. In the aesthetics of both the fixtures and the degree and type of light emitted, make both contribute to an ambience, geared to your market, that makes your models "feel" like a good place to live.

In effect, all of the Nuts & Bolts are tools of merchandising which will help create visual balance, good use of space and enhance presentation as well as architecture.

Think of the Nuts and Bolts as the mood makers that will help put home shoppers in the mood to BUY.

Staging is as important in models as it is in theatre. Wallpaper sets the mood and built-in window seating and bed arrangement provides cozy niches in this bedroom.

8

Accessories: Those Special Touches

The things we love the most find their way into our own homes. They become an extension of our personalities and a means of self expression.

It should be the same with model homes.

Models should be filled with things people ENJOY. Things that say something special about who could and should live here . . . things that add touches of surprise and delight.

ACCESSORIES are those special touches—the frosting on your merchandising cake. There's no easier way to breathe personality into interiors than through accessories. Plus, they provide inexpensive custom elements, and help prospects identify with models.

I'm convinced that little things mean a lot in transforming a model house into a "home".

A bowl of flowers, children's toys, bright table settings, pipes on a desk. These are the kinds of things that say your model homes are loving, cared-for, personal places to be. Instinctively, accessories can make people feel at home and at ease. They do so because they invite prospects to become involved.

Books and open magazines, for example, invite shoppers to thumb through the contents. I've seen prospects perusing the shelves of a bookcase, or examining colorful collections, and even picking up children's toys in models. It may be a colorful or remarkable accessory that provides the important memory link that helps a buyer recall your model later on, or leads him to walk across a room to investigate—and discover—special features in a model.

If you're not sure what accessories are, then go into your own home and list all the things that are not large pieces of furniture—plants, pictures, lamps, candlesticks, photos, momentos, collectables, kitchen gadgets and gimmicks—everything that says it's YOUR home.

Now, imagine your home without all those special touches. It would be a very sterile, lifeless, impersonal place. So are model homes that fail to address the life-injecting, personality-lending adjuncts of model merchandising: accessories. They are the finishing touches that turn a model house into a home.

Set tables with little luxuries like these to make a room special.

Make It Sparkle. The right accessory for a room is the one that "feels" good. It adds sparkle in the right place at the right time. Like a special ornament on a beautiful Christmas tree.

It's always fun to add an element of whimsy or fantasy in each model—and accessory items can be just what it takes to put smiles on faces. I like to tuck something with a childlike quality into a special nook or cranny—a whimsical cookie jar, crazy pillows, a heart shaped mirror, a Raggedy Ann doll or a wall plaque or needlepoint with quaint verse that might say something memorable. One of my favorite wall pieces was a graphic that read: "A frown is just a smile turned upside down." It caught the eye of just about everyone. And made them feel good too.

I feel that introducing a childlike quality into homes is a sure way to capture attention and win friends. We are all children at heart, though we sometimes become so sophisticated we lose touch with our feelings. A little whimsy often puts us back in touch with them.

That's why, though we tend to think of accessories as "things", I believe it is also important to think of them in terms of "feelings", special feelings they suggest to, and elicit from, your target market.

Use a Free Hand. Accessories belong everywhere. There's not a room or space in the model home that doesn't have need for it's own special touch—and I mean right down to the walk-in closets.

Hatboxes or an old trunk tucked inside closets to demonstrate shelf and storage space imply that every detail of your model—closets included—is designed with the buyer in mind.

Using various sized canned goods to demonstrate the spaciousness of a pantry, or placing pillows in storage or linen closet spaces to show off roominess, are also easy merchandising tricks that demonstrate builder concern for attention to detail.

Use a free hand in bathrooms with towels, toiletries, powder boxes and perfumes for "her", shaving gear, razor straps and grooming accessories for "him". In bedrooms, use accessories to say a boy, girl, teenager, baby or guests will sleep here.

Then go into living areas with items reflective of the family's interests: Games, stereo and electronic equipment, antiques, flower arrangements, books, pictures and graphics, pillows, ashtrays, candy jars, crafts and collectibles.

Beyond the knick knacks and personal effects that add description to your model home interiors, there are two design accessories that play a major role in merchandising. They are mirrors and plants. Let's take a look at them.

Accessories add personality to a theme punctuated by old-fashioned, hand-painted wall trim.

Mirrors: Reflect Good Taste. Mirrors are a popular accessory and a sure way to attract attention as well as direct traffic. People just naturally seem to head for a mirror and look in; it's almost a natural relfex.

A word of caution, however: Use mirrors honestly. As decorative splashes of excitement they become an asset. Used to create a false impression of spaciousness or to make up for a poorly planned space, they become a liability.

Today's sophisticated buyer may be very quick to perceive that you have used mirrors to make up for lack of space in a small room—and just as quick to perceive that it is a costly "bad trick" as well—one that would cost them dollars they may not want to spend.

Greenery: It's Great—But Don't Fake It. Plants are one of the most important accessories in model merchandising, but don't fake it at any cost! Because they are alive, lush and green, living plants bring models to life. And they've become a "way of life" for people. Since few homes today are without them, there's no excuse for not using plants plentifully in model homes.

And there's no excuse for using plastic substitutes. Honesty is always the best policy. However, when you use them, you must commit yourself to maintaining plants to look their best. Make sure to provide a salesman with a schedule for feeding and watering. Or employ a plant care service to look after them.

Plants play three important roles in merchandising model homes:
· They are accessories;
· they bring the outdoors "in";
· and they can be used to emphasize the coordination and flow of interior and exterior living spaces.

Use a light and sensible touch with plants. Don't inundate the model with so much greenery that your target buyers wonder if they've walked into a greenhouse rather than a model home.

Accessories in this room, my at-home office, are a record of special moments and special friends. I think the same joyous feelings can -- and should be -- conveyed in every model.

Seek And Ye Shall Find. The best accessories are often found in the most unlikely places.

It's a good idea to "explore" when you're ready to accessorize. I like to shop all over the world for accessories, and I'm always on the look out for tempting items that say, "buy Me!" I may not be able to use them right away for a specific job, but if an item says "special", I know I will use it eventually.

It pays to work with artists who enjoy their craft. They seem to produce the best work! Art fairs, craft shows and stores featuring handcrafted items are all good sources for distinctive accessory items. Here you're likely to find the kinds of items that your target buyer may collect himself, or create as his own hobby.

Be selective about accessories. Good accessorization is NOT buying large quantities of any one item to be stashed away on shelves and pulled off for later jobs in subsequent model home developments. It's selecting the right item that makes an appropriate statement in the room at hand. That wall graphic so perfect for today's wood and glass split level may not suit the Colonial model down the line.

Each project deserves an individual approach which means you must be creative in your search. You need to pay constant attention to marketing and merchandising trends—and know what's current in fashion and the home furnishings market, in particular.

Most important in your search for the right accessories is the research you've done before hand on your most likely buyers. You want to be on target with the market!

Remember, buyers identify most strongly when models are merchandised with a lived-in look as if they are the dwellings of a real family just like their own.

So refresh you memory. Go back and re-read your market family "profile"—the one we talked about in Chapter II. Remember those folks? You wrote out a script and described your family members in detail from age to hobbies and how each person spends his time.

Now is the time to re-read the script, or if you haven't written a complete one—finish it! Then you'll know what to buy to suit the lifestyle of the families your research has indicated are most likely to buy your homes.

Here's what I mean by a "lived-in" look; it's as though someone who lives in this home selected each item with loving care.

Tell A Story. Accessories should really say something personal about WHO your target buyer is.

Story-telling accessories can include trophies, awards, family pictures, sports gear, hobby paraphernalia, and collections of all kinds, proudly displayed in family rooms, bedrooms and kitchens. For example:

· Nothing sells a home to an amateur gardener like plants in abundance—in the bathrooms, living rooms and greenhouse windows; even potted herbs on the kitchen sink have special appeal.

· Wallpaper with a race car motif says "a boy lives in this room"; but accessories bring that boy to life— basketballs, footballs, a Little League cap, models and books tell us about him and what he likes to do.

· Who lives in the master suite? A couple who love each other. His after-shave and her cosmetics each have their own niche. Magazines and books are on shelves and tables. There may be a desk with her stationery and his books, or a bedside table with a porcelain coffee pot and two cups.

The items you choose may not always be exactly what your prospective customers might own, but if you've done your homework they'll be close enough to help them relate to the home and envision their own families living there.

If you hear a mother conclude that, "My teenager could be happy in this room"; or a father express delight in discovering a special room identified as his personal retreat because of the well-appointed executive desk—then you've done the job. You've sold them. You've helped them see how the home can function to meet their own needs.

100

Enough is Enough. A touch of surprise and delight is one thing. Clutter is another. So where do you stop? How do you recognize too much of a good thing?

Believe me, you CAN over accessorize! You can intimidate people. Knowing when to stop is one area that separates the "pro" from the non-professional and the gracious model from the garrish one.

Securing the advice of a professional merchandising expert can pay off not only in good results but in time and dollars saved and bottom line profits as well when it comes to accessories.

The professional has a critical eye, stays out front, is in constant communication with suppliers who create trend-setting products, and knows where to get the latest miracle materials or the fanciest antique hall tree. And more. A professional has learned to judge the right scale of accessories; which ones will contribute the right flavor and mood; how to get results, and when to stop!

So ask for advice when you need it. Many professional firms have a staff member called an "accessorizer" who devotes full-time to this crucial aspect of home merchandising.

However, for those who feel they have an "eye" for accessorization and want to give it a try, my rule of thumb is this: "Go for more quality and less quantity."

Give your buyers a touch of romance. Let them experience the warmth of your home. And make them feel comfortable. But take care not to overkill.

Accessories create interest here, without overwhelming.

102

The Mathematics, or, Budget Ahead.

The best interior results are the end product of a well-planned merchandising budget, and that budget should always take accessories into consideration.

As a rule of thumb, 18% of the merchandising budget can be comfortably allocated for accessories and should be.

There are some "tricks of the trade", however, for stretching dollars if you're tied to a low budget. Here are a few:

· Use large scale wall coverings to cut down the need for wall accessories. Plain walls obviously will require more decor.

· Know exactly how you want your walls and room to look upon completion, and where you want the buyers' eye to go first. Put your best accessories there.

· Stay with common colors. You'll have a wider variety of accessories to choose from at less cost.

Unless your project is in an upper price market, you may be wasting valuable dollars by purchasing expensive accessories that may not turn on your market anyway. Good merchandising is good accessorizing. But that does not necessarily mean high-priced accessories.

In the end, accessories are most important for what they contribute to the whole picture of your interior design. A visitor to your model homes may not be immediately aware of the accessorization. He may, in fact, not recall a single specific item. But you can be sure if it's done well he will remember that the home felt good; that he wanted to stay. And could and should be living there. Now that's clever accessorizing!

9

Create Male Places In All The Right Spaces.

Elsie De Wolfe was a remarkable and often quoted English actress, hostess and decorator who enchanted the world with her ideas on interiors and entertaining. She once said that It's the personality of the woman that the home expresses. Men are forever guests in the home, no matter how much happiness they may find there.

With due respect to the late Ms. De Wolfe, more and more men today are taking an interest in the way the interiors of their homes look—right along with finding happiness in them.

As they write out deposit checks on new homes they are also casting a careful glance towards special nooks and crannies they can call their own within the dwelling place.

What today's man is looking for are special little retreats

It's HIS castle, so make him feel at home. The male side of the buying team deserves rooms designed just for _him_. Like this one.

and hideaways for mellowing out after a hard day's work earning the mortgage payment: libraries, dens, hobby and work rooms, for instance.

He is seeking new and different entertainment centers—rooms that cater to party needs and space to house the burgeoning new electronic media flooding the market.

And, he has an eye on the kitchen, where burly quarterbacks as well as females are as likely to be seen today in pursuit of a perfect quiche or beef en croute. As Emily Post said, woman accepted cooking as a chore, but man has turned it into recreation.

Merchandising lets the home-buying male know that your homes can fill his recreational needs and all others—through the best looking, most efficient kitchens, dens, libraries, wine cellars, media rooms, bedrooms, baths, recreational and exercise centers he's ever stepped foot into.

And good merchandising keeps in mind that a large corps of today's male buyers are <u>single</u> males with definite ideas about how today's bachelor pad—be it city condominium or suburban home—should size up.

It's easy to create male places in all the right spaces, if you take a look at what interests the majority of the male, shelter-buying public.

Bold patterns
and sturdy
texture make
a man feel
comfortable in
this room.

Map Out a Media Room. A sure way to seize interest of the male side of the buying team is with an attention-grabbing media room.

The Media Room is futurism in the here-and-now. It's stocked with all those fascinating electronic gadgets from the latest audio-visual equipment to extravagant big-screen television. A home computer, home-movie and slide projectors and home-viewing screens might be thrown in for good measure.

Few males, single or married, are able to resist the intrigue of an electrifying electronics room in their very own homes. You're liable to inspire electronic geniuses of the future as well. Children and teenagers will delight in the idea of the push-button magic such a room provides.

There are many ways to merchandise the coming age of advanced electronics in your models. If a complete media room seems out of line with your particular product, combine the idea with a family room or living room. Or turn a section of your model home's Great Room into a multi-media electronics corner.

What you don't see in the other side of the room which has a disco dance floor and wet bar, perfect for parties.

108

Massage The Sensuous Zones. A home, alas, must be more than an electronics workshop to today's man, however. It should be a haven that's comfortable, safe and even something more—it can be sensuous too.

Model homes should have sex appeal. Afterall, people buy homes with their hearts as well as their heads, and that includes men as well as women.

There are more ways to merchandise sex appeal in a model home than you might think. You can merchandise the sensuous "zones"—create sybaritic baths and sensuous spas. You can merchandise romance in fireplaces and fireside conversation pits, atriums, lavish master suites and well-appointed dressing areas with plenty of room for a man and man-sized needs.

One sure way to play up the sensuous aspects of design and decor in these areas is to make the most of luxury and luxury items. Fantastic finishing materials, such as slick mosaic and ceramic tiles, marvelous marbles, plush carpeting, and the tantalizing appeal of polished gold, lustrous copper and other metalics used as sharp contrast to rich redwood or walls of glimmering mirror and glass doors, windows, shower stalls and skylights . . . all can be very sensuous!

One of the most sensuous rooms I've ever experienced was a seductive bath designed by California architect Barry Berkus. We merchandised Berkus' room with a rich interplay of textures. You'll see the results pictured here.

This bath was merchandised to make the most of the artistic architecture—beamed and vaulted ceiling, a sunken conversation pit with fireplace and spacious shower overlooking a generous greenhouse grotto.

111

Appeal To All Five Senses. Sensuous merchandising, really, is appealing to all five senses—taste, vision, touch, sound and smell.

The way to a man's heart may be through his stomach, but you can excite his interest in your model homes with a visual excitement and direct appeal to the senses of sound and touch as well.

Much has already been said about visual appeal, the first and most important "sense" in the sense of merchandising. Visual merchandising is the decorator's most potent weapon—color, texture, scale and contrast are the ammunition.

But what about the sense of smell? It can be merchandised too. Here are two ways to make your models smell good:

· Use dried flower arrangements that have a soft pleasing fragrance. Most noteworthy among the dried florals for aroma is eucalyptus. The scent can be subdued but enchanting and woodsy in a model.

· Herbs—blooming fresh in a greenhouse window—or in dried arrangements are another possibility to consider.

Next, consider sound. Certainly the sound of recorded music playing throughout the home will bring your models to life. More important, you can add some of the sounds of life. For example:

· a crackling fire;
· trickling water in a fountain;
· birds in an atrium.

Sound isn't fundamental to sales, but sounds can be fun and can help emphasize special features or a theme.

Sound played an important role in one of the most elaborate themed projects I worked on, based on a "Great Movies" theme. Each model had a movie theme such as "Gone With The Wind" and "Pillow Talk" and each was decorated accordingly. To add to the specialized theme, sound-tracks from each movie were played in the models. It was a small touch that delighted home shoppers and made the models a more memorable adventure. Men in particular, seemed to notice and appreciate the music in the background.

The sense of taste is obviously the most difficult to deal with in merchandising models, but you can appeal to the male buyers' sense of taste in a suggestive way. A well-accessorized country kitchen can almost make you smell the aroma of freshly baked bread. And nothing sells an amateur gourmet cook like a kitchen stashed with all the right utensils, equipment and gadgetry. The man in your market will know this would be a perfect place for pursuing culinary interests.

Male places go outside the model house as well as inside. Consider barbeque centers or sundecks and garages big eough to accommodate "shop" equipment and tool cabinets. Think about special dark rooms for photography; pool rooms, hobby rooms or basement rooms converted for his pleasure.

Male places are successful merchandising messages when they tell the man of the house there's no place like home—especially when it's your home, the one you built just for HIM.

A few carefully selected accessories are often enough to tag a room to male interests.

10

Make The Kitchen Appetizing.

It isn't a place just for cooking anymore. Nor the sole domain of mom, visited occasionally by hungry youngsters or midnight snackers. Today's kitchen is the heart of the household.

Probably no other room in the home has been affected more by Americans' changing lifestyles than the kitchen. Be it tempting tidbit or tasty spread, opened into a family room or a room unto itself, the kitchen is <u>still</u> the room where a majority of your home-buyers are going to really "live".

So merchandise its livability! Make the kitchen a main course in your marketing menu. Merchandise it to be a light, bright, warm and inviting, happy, hospitable place that will convey to buyers its pleasures and potentials. The ingredients for kitchen merchandising success are color, surface coverings, emphasis on space

It's liveable as well as functional. Here, food could be prepared among family and friends in a welcome setting.

and amenities, accessories and appliances. You'll want to serve them up in a banquet of good taste.

Once again, you'll want to tune into your particular market. Some market segments may turn on to different merchandising techniques in kitchens.

Empty nesters, for instance, tend to favor easy on-the-eye soft colors such as yellows, greens and blues, and are receptive to touches of drama, sophistication and elegance. They are, after all, in the position at last to seek out their "dream house" and "dream kitchens".

The singles and young couples or family markets are likely to be split in their preferences. Part may prefer a "status" kitchen, merchandised for parties and gourmet cooking, while the other part may be grateful for very functional and informal kitchen treatment, designed with practicality in mind. Once you've sized up your market—you can size up your kitchen design and adapt merchandising strategies that will meet the needs of both.

Color It Bright. For a long time, well into the '50s, it seemed as if every kitchen was composed of institutional white counters and appliances against an occasional backdrop of pastels.

Later, in the '60s, someone discovered color, but in a limited palette. Very limited. Avocado green and harvest gold soon became the major colors in the kitchen rainbow.

Finally, however, the limited color spell was broken. Yesterday's kitchens, slumbering in the shadow of limited hues were put to rest, and today everything's coming up brilliant color. From counter materials to floor and wall coverings, fabrics and appliances—there's an unlimited medley of kitchen hues from sunny, warm yellows to robust reds, jaunty blues and fresh greens, brilliant combinations and bright plaids, prints and patterns in wallpapers that set a colorful mood.

With the exception of a few outrageous shades, there's scarcely a color that can't be appetizingly used in the creation of an irresistable kitchen.

There are almost no steadfast rules in color merchandising, but there are some basic guidelines that, if followed like a recipe, will almost guarantee a delectable kitchen and sizzling sales. They are:

· Keep the kitchen cheerful, warm and bright. Too much deep, strong color can overpower. Save those deeply sensuous tones for the bed and bath or use them as kitchen accents in a balanced combination with lighter, brighter shades and neutrals.

· Be careful with deep, dark colors when selecting counter materials. Most people prefer—and relate to—the look of light, clean color in kitchen counter tops.

· Consider lighter woods and veneers for cabinetry—they expand visual space—a plus in large as well as small kitchens.

· Very bright, vivid colors such as the neon oranges and hot shocking pinks seem to "rev up" people and emotions. This is why you see them in fastfood establishments in which quick turnaround is desired. Don't let them dominate your kitchens or you may find prospects "rushing" through.

· Light wall and floor coverings make the small kitchen seem larger and warmer. Even when wall surface is at an absolute minimum, nothing can introduce color and warmth like wallpaper. Wallpapering ceilings as well as walls will visually expand the space of the kitchen.

· If there is one color scheme that is almost a shoe-in as a universal kitchen favorite it's the "naturals look" that uses warm earth tones and natural materials such as wood, burls and fibers, textured counter laminates in wood finishes, and rich wood cabinetry. You can add interest and accent with colorful accessories.

· Keep in mind that lighting will affect the colors you choose. Warm deluxe tubes in luminous kitchen ceilings give a cozier feeling than the regular fluorescent lights and minimize the risk of an unattractive blue or green "tinge".

· Very large or country kitchens are often a greater challenge than the small, efficiency-type kitchen. Here, there's plenty of space to utilize color, texture and accessories to demonstrate the many activities to which a large kitchen is suited. However, it's important to "divide" such space subtly. You can use an area rug to cut down an expanse of hard floor surface, and with complimenting changes in wall coverings and furnishings, to introduce warm, cozy color and texture that demarks work areas and eating space.

Remember, the kitchen that "opens" into a family room or dining room needs careful merchandising. A balance needs to be struck between a visual continuity and the use of space. Generally, it's best to provide backgrounds of wall and floor surfaces with color continuity and to use accessories to mark changes in room use.

It's a breakfast room, but with a quick change of accessories, it's also a game table and a family gathering place.

How do you create a living room in the kitchen?....

Yellow lets the sun shine in. Collectibles add a feeling of residency. A mock window of mirrored panes adds extra light and dimension.

The Spice That's Right. The well merchandised kitchen is as much a "living room" as a cooking room. And accessories are one way to demonstrate the livability of the space.

They convey warmth, feelings of hominess and "teach" the would-be buyer how little things—a built-in spice rack, shelves for cookbooks or a menu center or desk unit, for instance—can be used to customize a kitchen to family lifestyle.

Some successful accessorization ideas that can help you spice up your kitchens might include:

· Personalizing small kitchens with collections, canisters or gourmet cookbooks to give a feeling of warmth and residence when there's no room for chairs, table or larger pieces of furniture.

· If light is a problem in a small windowless kitchen, you can create a "window" with rectangles of mirror that are "framed" and paned with molding and draped to look like the real thing. The reflective quality of the mirror will provide extra illumination.

· If the kitchen is large enough for a three-star chef, emphasize the generous size with utensils, durable foodstuffs, condiment racks or bottle holders that demonstrate spaciousness.

· If, on the other hand, counter space is a a premium, show your potential buyer how effectively space can be used in this way: Use stackable accessories and racks and holders that are built-in or attached to walls.

Keep small counter areas free (less is sometimes more) to show that the space has been planned for maximum efficiency and value.

• There are some special touches that add little to the budget but are worth their weight in gold in both large and small kitchens, such as:

    – bottle and condiment racks built into pantry doors;

    – stemware racks in cabinets;

    – and merchandising with canned goods to demonstrate pantry capacity.

If these merchandising "garnishes" are invisible without opening doors, invite the househunter to open up and take a look inside with inviting labels that say, "Open Me!"

Make It Look Easy. The career women in your home shopping audience—both working mothers and childless professionals— will especially appreciate kitchens that are streamlined for efficiency. Think of this sub-market as you plan kitchen merchandising strategy.

Arrange up-to-date equipment in efficient arrangements or easy-to-see storage bins for these convenience-minded prospects. Make the most of storage areas. And merchandise plentiful pantries or special cabinets for maximum exposure. Fill them with appropriate items to demonstrate size and space.

You may also want to provide built-ins for silver, flatware, glass and crystal to demonstrate kitchen "potential" when storage space is short, or when large space permits extra storage.

Shelves for cookbooks and a desk for menu planning and household accounting are little extras most homebuyers like to see. You can also add tray storage and stemware racks in assorted degree of elaborateness. And flowerboxes for plants or potted herbs.

There are other inexpensive extras that add to kitchen charm and convenience. A blackboard or corkboard for family "information" is one example. Collections of copper molds, cups, old plates and color canisters and crockery give kitchens a "lived-in" look. And the latest counter-top push-button appliances can turn an ordinary kitchen into a cook's paradise.

Futuristic products tell prospects your kitchens focus on tomorrow.

Orbit Into The Space Age. Every builder and merchandiser who hopes to maintain a competitive edge on the market will want to keep an eye on the future and forward-thinking technology that almost daily is revolutionizing kitchens and cooking.

Frankly futuristic accessories for kitchens and cooking became auspiciously commonplace with the microwave oven. And, almost as fast as you can say computer read-out, new items are coming on line—many of which are likely to become standardized features in model homes in the near future.

Convection ovens and high-speed food processors controlled by computer chips are available now. The computer chip, which stores information in a tiny space, holds promise for sophisticated data processing—as well as food processing—in kitchens. Futurists say we can look forward to home computers that may someday make instant conversions in recipes from standard measurements to metric, store recipes, convert them to different yields, keep track of our grocery purchases, of money spent, and tell us when we're out of certain items.

As a center of the household, the kitchen is where new products and new trends such as these can and should be merchandised with sizzle. Your home shoppers will find them fun and fascinating. Keep in mind that kitchens are ideal places to offer food for thought and fulfill the promise of a better tomorrow with a full-fledged marketing menu.

Tell your prospects what's new, what's good and what's coming, and chances are good they'll come and get it while it's hot!

11

Bathrooms: Make a Big Splash.

Bathrooms, for a long time, were considered little more than a necessity. Bath fixtures, like dishwashers or water heaters, were simply "standard equipment" put in place by indifferent builders who paid little attention to detail and design. The results were decidedly dull, frankly boorish baths.

Then important groups of homebuyers, namely singles, young couples and empty nesters, began to demand more. More space. More luxury. More excitement. Increasingly attuned to the pleasures of sunken tubs and hydrojets, whirlpools, saunas, and other sybaritic amenities, these new bath enthusiasts helped wash indifferent attitudes down the drain. Builders caught on. And the bathroom blossomed. Today the bath that makes a big splash is a key sales factor in model homes, second only to kitchens in

The rule for bathrooms is: there are no rules except to make the bath a welcome retreat with plenty of eye-catching, visual appeal.

buyer appeal. No other room offers such potential for merchandising sheer extravagance. Or for merchandising color, texture and surface "wrappings" as the Bath.

Remember in merchandising your homes that the bathroom is no longer just a "necessity". It has become a family health "spa", an exercise and physical fitness room, a beauty retreat, a lavish center of luxury away from the workday world. Above all, the best-selling bathrooms epitomize relaxation and escape.

Smart-looking surface covers from patterned wallpaper and wood cabinetry to stained glass windows enliven a large bathroom.

Customize and Glamorize. In order to meet consumer demand for better baths, architects, builders and merchandisers are thinking custom and glamour right from the beginning in terms of design construction and amenities. They're planning sensuous, seductive, charming, cozy, alluring and sumptuous as well as "efficient" baths.

How? By alloting more space to bathing comfort in new homes, for one thing. The boxy bath of yesteryear is lofty and open today, thanks to sky-lights and vaulted ceilings, plenty of glass, level changes and additional square footage. Landscaped atriums or greenhouse grotto-like areas add to the grandeur.

And increasingly, the "standard" equipment—showers and toilets—are being put in small adjoining compart-ments, to separate them from lavish bathing retreat areas.

Even when space is tight, luxury can be afforded in baths through design ingenuity (custom cabinetry for exam-ple), through special effects (creative lighting, mirrored walls and ceramic tiles, etc.), new shapes (in tubs, sinks, toilets and showers), built-in features and particularly through the unlimited supply of innovative bath amenities that can transform dreary into delightful.

There's such an infinite variety of fixtures and accessories available today it's no wonder the bath has emerged as the "glamour" room of many new homes. With the wide variety of choice and price range, there's no reason every builder can't or shouldn't merchandise at least one exciting bathroom, be his project a lower-priced development or a high-priced custom home.

In lower-priced homes, the fancy details can include charming double basins, walls of mirror, glass shower stalls, new molded sinks, tubs, toilets and showers (in a rainbow of colors) special built-ins or unusual cabinetry and sparkling tiles or other highly tex-tured wall and floor coverings, finishing materials and fixtures that sell visual excitement. The earthy green lushness of plants in profusion will add to the sensuous appeal of every bath.

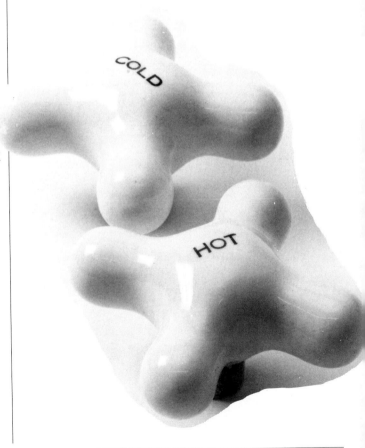

Think Big And Beautiful. In higher-priced houses, the sky is the limit for extravagance in the bathing chamber, from sun-drenching skylights to colorful atriums, fireplaces and conversation pits, right down to the smallest details—gold plated fixtures or even a solid gold sink (they're available!). This is the best room in your model to merchandise self-indulgence. So think big and beautiful.

The most lavish baths are richly appointed and seductive. Built-in whirlpools and hydrojets can be included as standard features. And the bathtub itself can range from fanciful, old-fashioned footed models that have nostalgic appeal to Romanesque marble models sunk low in plush carpeting, or revolutionary molded shapes with recessed neck rests and molded nooks for soaps and toiletries.

You'll want to create areas of interest to make the bathroom environment interesting. A bath-turned spa is sure to have appeal to fitness enthusiasts. Add an exercise or ballet bar, a hot tub or sauna. Manufacturers are also now offering completely controlled environment enclosures—the ultimate for post-exercise relaxation that fit nicely into spa rooms. These "enclosures" provide soothing cyles of sun, steam and showers. You can merchandise them to illustrate potential in luxury.

Wildest dreams and wildest design notions are possible—and permissible—in model home bathrooms. So explore them.

Amenities and accessories can mean the difference between "everyday" and "distinctive" baths. Sun lamps, and steam machines are good ways to beef-up bathroom merchandising. So are customized fixtures that range from fluted, gilded hardware designs to sophisticated chrome or old-world antique reproductions.

Baths are getting bigger and better. And the more sizzle you merchandise, the better your chances to sell.

In fact I recommend going a step beyond the conventional. Add charisma to a small space with stainless steel paneling that enlarges and enlightens. Encourage prospects to think expansively. Add bookshelves and turn the bath into a reading library. Add stereo equipment, telephones, and how about a wet bar near the sauna?

You name it—today, anything and everthing goes in the all-purpose bathroom. It's the homeowner's place to retreat, regroup and relax. And don't let him forget how much better it can be in the homes you have to offer.

A romantic,
footed tub
with nostalgic
overtones takes
center stage
in this
splendid setting.

Black is
beautiful.
Need I say
more!

12

Design Small Spaces To Live Big.

Less can be more, or at least look and feel like more. It's true! There's a lot more going for small spaces than builders and buyers often realize. Properly merchandised, the exciting potential of small rooms—their efficiency, easier maintenance, warmth, charm, intimacy and coziness—can pack greater, sales-oriented wallop than the huge room that is sometimes, frankly a lot of wasted space.

Since rising costs in both land and materials may dictate less square footage and smaller rooms in more and more future developments, sales-conscious builders are asking how to make the most of reduced floor plan dwelling units.

The solution is simple: You can merchandise those small spaces for excitement and watch LESS space grow into MORE sales. The answer does not lie in merely slapping

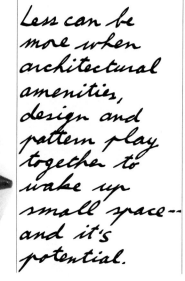

Less can be more when architectural amenities, design and pattern play together to wake up small space—and it's potential.

light colored paint on walls or sticking in a few small pieces of furniture that leave prospects with less than they want, however.

Nor do you want to deceive. Today's homebuyers will quickly recognize a ruse in the form of underscale furniture and floor-to-ceiling mirrors. Both are unrealistic approaches. The best way to deal with small space is to accept the challenge!

Merchandise small spaces to illustrate their potential for intimacy and efficiency. Show how small rooms can be used in a variety of ways and excite prospects with the realization that the small room will indeed accommodate that new stereo unit, the big screen TV, the inherited baby grand piano—and all of the important and favorite things the homebuyer will want to bring into his new residence.

Regardless of the small space in question, there are those familiar "basics" of design, color, lighting, furnishings, textures and accessorization that apply across the board.

But, before we talk about these fundamentals, let's take a step all the way back to the beginning and start with architecture.

An early consultation between architect, builder and merchandiser before construction begins may result in refinements that bring intrinsic interest to small areas and mitigate potential problems.

A small room grows in size and stature with a wall of multi-faced built-ins.

The placement of doors, the size, shape and placement of windows and fireplaces, the inclusion of skylights or greenhouse and atrium windows, window seats, additional nooks, level changes, dividers in place of solid walls—these type of architectural elements can give small spaces "built-in" excitement. And a professional interior merchandiser may be able to suggest where they'll work best in your small space schemes.

A good builder will also be market-conscious in the initial planning stage. Singles may be attracted by unusual floor plans, older couples might tend to avoid stairs, sunken rooms and may prefer separate dining areas. Built-in entertainment centers may appeal to younger folks, while efficiency and low maintenance ideas will lure the older set. So take these essentials into consideration before you move on to the next step of:

Pattern adds punch in small doses in a small room. But keep patterns on a small scale.

Color. Be monochromatic but not monotonous with color. By keeping wall and floor covering, window treatments and major furnishings within a one color family, the small space will tend to "flow" and feel larger.

You can use texture to add interest—light colored wainscotting that melds with a floor covering of the same tone, for instance.

Remember that the eye will stop at every color and pattern change. So keep wall covering patterns subtle. And use bright colors judiciously as accents. They pop out at the eye and, in excess, may visually reduce space.

Lighting. Small space merchandising exploits all sources of light. Well designed and well placed windows and skylights are the best sources and they permit the merchandiser to create an "expanded" room by coordinating the indoor/outdoor environments.

So be sure to open up window spaces, keep glass free of obstruction and bring curtain panels just to the edge of the window for maximum light. Reflect the light and outdoor view that is available by backing shelves, bookcases and clear glass shelves with mirror—even china cabinets and closets will benefit from this kind of light-reflecting treatment.

Another illuminating idea for small areas is to introduce theatrical lighting. Or demonstrate how mood, character and atmosphere can be easily altered through special indirect or track lighting fixtures and recessed lighting in ceilings and built-in units.

Furnishings. The key to furnishing small spaces is to use light-scale, not small scale furniture.

Queen Anne, open-back and caneback chairs in standard sizes integrate beautifully in smaller spaces. So do light scale chrome, glass and lucite, armless designs and pieces that are "open" with delicate legs, open backs and arms.

Fabrics for furnishings serve small room purposes best when they meld with the wall and floor coverings' initial monochromatic theme. The contrast of dark in large pieces—say a dark green sofa—against a light background will reduce the feeling of spaciousness and your efforts to enhance room size.

It's a good idea to use "double duty" furnishings—hide-a-beds; butcher block tables that double as working surfaces or breakfast bars; chaise lounges that can be made into beds; and built-ins such as wall units or shelves that serve as storage as well as display cases, entertainment centers and desks.

The benefits of double duty furnishings are two-fold: The concept has a strong sales message as well as a practical function because it demonstrates to the house hunter just how versatile and livable small rooms and spaces can be.

When pulling your furnishings together, keep in mind these thoughts:

· Keep furniture in small places as interesting, versatile and practical as possible.

· Show the buyer how his old pieces—Grandma's sideboard, for example—can be accommodated into the home, when possible.

· Avoid a monotonous atmosphere by using "matching everything" furniture against a monochromatic color scheme. A few color and pattern variations in upholstery are important for avoiding a plain vanilla look.

Openness adds spaciousness to small spaces but be sensitive to the use of color and patterns so that everything blends from room to room.

Accessories. Accessories are like adjectives to describe the ideal lifestyle that can be enjoyed in a room or house, and scale is the key to their effective use in small areas.

A little bit of bright color in a couple of small throw pillows creates visual excitement. But a heavy, large painting in an oversized wood frame can destroy the intimacy of a cozy room.

It's better to scale down the size of the painting and use a delicate frame, or a grouping of several small pictures, than to reiterate the smallness of a room with a large, dominant accessory.

Too many groupings of too many small accessories may add up to clutter. And too much color contrast or dominating, large accessories will upset the room's proportion and destroy its warmth and romance.

Ideas To Try. Interestingly, many successful builders find that their "big" spaces pack more emotional punch and sell better when merchandised to feel more intimate. This tells us there is a substantial market for very appealing small spaces, if we "show off" these areas to best advantage.

Here are some showcasing ideas that can work successfully for your smallest rooms and homes:

· Horizontal wood siding in a light or mellow color, wrapped up a wall can give a room amazing depth.

· So can the continuation of a floor covering—say a ceramic tile or light parquet—all the way up a wall.

· A small master bathroom can be every bit as exciting as a cavernous one when skylights, large windows and clear glass enclosures are integrated into design.

· The creation of a hobby center or study in the closet of a small secondary bedroom, underscored by recessed lighting, demonstrates the potential of a limited floor plan.

· Contrasting textures—in wallpapers, flooring, fabrics and surface coverings—save a monochromatic room from monotony and appeals to the visual sense.

· Built-in seating units with storage space underneath, framed by a high window, expands the floor space in a tiny room.

· And finally, create VPPs—Very Private Places—wherever you can.

Save space with a storage bed and a wall of shelving. Prospects love ideas they can adapt themselves.

142

Very Private Places. Every prospective buyer is a VIP—a Very Important Person—and one way to emphasize the point, particularly in small spaces, is to create VPPs (Very Private Places) that tell would-be-buyers your models are special despite the mathematics of the floor plans.

VPPs are personal, private retreats, quiet zones and corners within the closed-in walls of small space dwelling units. They are specifically merchandised to demonstrate that privacy, seclusion, security, warmth and romance do not have to be sacrificed when floor space is reduced.

They can be created by the architect—window seats, skylights in a kitchen work area, pitched ceilings for dramatic impact, greenhouse windows in a kitchen, or quiet niches between rooms or in hallways.

They also can be created by the merchandiser—built-in units for collections, study spaces, play areas, toy storage, a hobby area in a secondary bedroom, a special seating arrangement by the fire for reading, private his and her compartments for work or hobbies in the master suite . . . the list is almost endless. Remember to think in terms of entire rooms or units as well as spaces within them. For example:

· A small home, condominium or apartment—merchandised as a "bachelor pad" with lots of solid color, texture, a dose of sex appeal and plenty of built-ins becomes a VPP.

· A very small living room can be given VPP status through use of finished paneling with batten treatment on one wall and matching wainscotting on others, personalizing the area with tasteful design.

· A child's room, a very small secondary bedroom, becomes a fantasy VPP when the bed is positioned in a corner against a low window allowing space for built-in shelves and toy bins cut out like cages. These provide storage as well as play space in the larger-feeling room.

VPP treatment will mark a room, space or unit as a personal private retreat and give it a very cozy glow.

I've found that this kind of merchandising does double duty. It demonstrates the cozy, human scale of small spaces, and their versatility as well. Perhaps most important, it puts smiles on buyers' faces, and their all important deposits on your small space units!

What could be more fun or convenient than storage space in a zoo motif?

13

Add Some Fun Spots.

Walt Disney was a remarkable success and a beloved American hero because he appealed to the "child" in all of us.

He catered to our fantasies, gave us something to smile about and enriched our lives with childlike pleasures. Not only did he remind us to "stop and smell the roses along the way", he provided countless delightful and whimsical avenues for doing so.

There's a valuable merchandising lesson in Mr. Disney's irresistible, forever young-at-heart approach to living. Certainly we must address ourselves to the serious side of our home building industry—to the need for integrity and quality in the shelter-producing field. But there's no reason we can't generate a little fun, in the Disney tradition, along the way, is there? After all, who said homes have to be all formality?

Extra bedrooms become ideal fun zones when merchandised with popular trends in mind...

Needless to say, you will want to provide home shoppers with gracious, formal living areas when they want and demand them.

But give them some excitement too. Merhandise some bright, "fun spots" that beckon prospects to a life of recreation, casual relaxation, retreat, hobby and crafts and some down-home, family good times.

This kind of merchandising can work wonders for sales, profits and the most mundane floorplans.

Ordinary book-shelves become an adventure when dressed up with an aviation motif.

A Place to "Kick Back". "Fun spots" are the nooks, corners, crannies, special areas or even entire rooms—that can be merchandised to turn serious faces into smiling ones. They tell prospects your homes are designed for good times. They're better than aspirin! They should ease the mind, soothe the spirit, settle the nerves and suggest to your would-be buyers that "Here's a place to kick off your shoes and enjoy yourself and your family".

A bonus room turned into a "pool room" with pool table, old time pictures, tiffany shades and a walk-up/sit down bar is the kind of thing I'm talking about. Doesn't that sound a lot more appealing than an oversized room stuffed with attractive furniture but no potential for fun? Other "fun spot" ideas you might consider could include:

· A family entertainment center with a big screen TV and a popcorn machine.

· A wetbar-cum-soda fountain with ice cream parlor style table and chairs in a bonus room.

· A teenager's room that converts into a disco lounge.

· A safari room filled with hunters' trophies and treasures (in place of an everyday den)

· Or a wall of shelves reflecting a variety of hobbies—models, trains, sports trophies, dolls or decoy ducks in family areas.

· A music room for practice of family sing-alongs or orchestrating musical interludes.

· If there's not room for the piano elsewhere—how about tucking it into a den or bedroom?

· A potter's wheel in a bright sunroom might be a hobbist's idea of fun.

· Or an oversized aquarium or other special places for pets might appeal to animal lovers.

· A treehouse will mean "fun" to someone, certainly.

· And so will special animated built-ins—in a zoo theme or cowboy motif—in kids' rooms (for climbing, storage and fantasizing).

Dens, sitting rooms, family and bonus rooms, secondary bedrooms, lofts, solariums or greenhouse rooms, spas and atriums, basements and even attics are all likely candidates for "fun spot" treatment. But look to unlikely, hard-to-use spaces as well. A long hall can become a gallery for special collections of prints or family photos and memorabilia.

Another wall, say near the garage, might be tapped for hanging tennis racquets and ski equipment and become your sports center. You can use large, colorful hooks or an old fashioned wall-type hatrack for the hardware.

Current trends can be adapted to "fun spots". I know at least one marketing director with a California building firm who always insists that the decorator/merchandiser design at least one bedroom in a model after the current movie or popular fad such as the Superman craze or roller disco. These bedrooms are always a center of attention in the model complexes and you can be sure home shoppers remember them—and the model homes in which they're discovered. One included a lifesize superman doll in a telephone booth in a child's room.

How many cats do you see? Part of the fun is discovering them all.

My own favorite "fun spots" include a teenager's bedroom designed by my staff to convert into a disco lounge/party room. We put in bubble gum lamps, an art deco palm tree with decorative Tivoli lights, a big screen TV, a "Bijou Theatre" sign in neon lights, a stereo system and plenty of records to give it a party room personality. It was a room totally geared to having fun that happened to serve as a place for sleeping as well.

We used the disco theme in a bonus room in another development. By day, the room was a typical family activity center. But at night, theatrical lighting converted it into a party/dance room.

We built in a wetbar and soda fountain, screens for viewing family movies and slides, and stocked shelves and tables with electronic games. The costs were not excessive, but the result demonstrated a multi-use potential for the room and gave prospects ideas for personalizing their own homes for family fun.

A Few "Favorite Things". I've found that shoppers always appreciate merchandising that demonstrates how space within a home can function in different ways. Particularly if it contributes to a more exciting lifestyle and to indulgence in our favorite pastimes.

We are, after all, living in a society that is putting greater emphasis—in both time and money—on leisurely and recreational pursuits. Good merchandising will show prospective buyers how a model will contribute to both. For example, almost everyone will enjoy discovering a special room designated for doing his favorite things or turning his hand at some form of self-expression or creative hobby. Extra bedrooms are ideal for this, and merchandised in such a way, can help promote sales of larger floor plans.

Any mother who loves to sew but hates the hassle of hunting up patterns, sewing kit, unraveled spools of thread from assorted drawers and retrieving scissors from the kids—will delight in the idea of a special place designated as a sewing area where she won't have to play hide-and-seek with supplies. It might be a sewing room, or a closet converted into a sewing center.

The same theory can be applied to other hobbies—a painter's studio, a model builder's den, photographer's studio—or just about any kind of craft center. You can merchandise secondary

bedrooms for these purposes by adding built-ins and shelving units for storage and display. Provide work counters and lighting techniques that make them convenient, workable and practical.

Possibilities for merchandising "fun spots" and the "good life" will vary from coast to coast and market to market. In colder climates you may want to make the most of basements and rumpus rooms by turning them into party rooms, wine cellars, year round greenhouses, collectors' dens or childrens' play zones. Make your goal one that will enchant browsers with innovative approaches to indoor "fun".

In California and other warm-weather climates where jogging, cycling and exercise are year-round pursuits, the exercise room has reached new levels of popularity. We see them more and more in model homes, too.

A word of advice, however, if you plan to merchandise an exercise room: make it warm, appealing, and inviting! That means doing more than stocking it with cold institutional looking exercise equipment. You'll want to add color and "fun" super graphics on walls, colorful cartoons of exercise enthusiasts, perhaps, and plenty of bright color on walls and floors to suggest that the room can be as much fun as hard work!

If you create a hobby room or crafts studio, reinforce the idea as part of the lifestyle of the home. For example, if you merchandise a quilting or sewing room—use quilts on walls or needlepoint as seat coverings elsewhere to suggest that the things done in this room for fun, contribute to the personality of the entire home.

A home gardener's favorite specimen of flowers and plants blooming in an atrium can show up in every room.

If you create a photographer's studio—use blownup and enlarged photographs as artwork in other rooms throughout the house.

Keep On Going . . . Remember that "fun spots" can go outdoors, too. Patios, barbeque pits, gazebos in various sizes—from those just big enough for a bench for two to those large enough to cover a dance floor—outdoor wetbars, spas, swimming pools, miniature putting greens and enchanting Japanese gardens with fish ponds and narrow curving walkways—all of these add to a model homes' potential for good times and good living. If only we could throw in an amusement park carousel or a riverboat ride to make them all the more enchanting!

It would be great fun, indeed, to incorporate Disneyland fantasy in the form of Sleeping Beauty's castles, "trips" into Tomorrowland and exotic space-aged paraphernalia into our lives, but practical model home merchandising may not be ready yet for such extremes in the "fun spot" department.

We'll have to stick with more practical "at-home" kinds of ideas. And certainly there are plenty within the realm of practicality to be explored and tested.

As long as we make the endeavor to provide home shoppers with the kinds of environments that fulfill at least some of their fantasies and most of their needs we'll be on the right track. Builders who do these things in their models—and make them fun besides—will be on the track to increased sales and profits.

Keep the kids home, or enjoy a romantic interlude. Both ideas go in this disco/dance room.

14

Making The Most of Nostalgia.

The maxim, "They don't build 'em like they used to" may be true enough, but in a positive rather than negative sense. Contemporary builders tuned into space planning, bold new architecture and new-fangled products have improved the quality of homes and living.

Nevertheless, a great many home buyers today seem to yearn for the way things "used to be". Old is popular.

Old buildings are being restored rather than razed. In new construction, elements of older, period design are in demand. Hand craftmanship has achieved new respect. And as fast as new products that look "old" are introduced, they're grabbed up in hot cakes fashion. What's more, period furnishings, antiques and the "country look" are more popular than ever. Clearly, we're a people infatuated with nostalgia.

Memories are made in rooms like this one. Country stripes, starched eyelit and momentoes are reminescent of Grandmother's day.

And there's no place where its presence can be more influential—or appreciated—than in new model homes.

I really believe a sprinkling of nostalgia—sepia photographs, antique china or a table or hutch like Grandma used to have, for example—adds warmth to the polish and shine of brand new models.

Frankly, too much "newness" can sometimes feel fake to prospects. Even perfection has its flaws. I know from experience, both in merchandising interiors and in observing homebuyers, that it is not necessarily perfection—perfect furnishings, perfect taste and exquisite detail—luxury or even function that sells homes. Often it is something harder to define and even more elusive to capture.

It has to do with a mood, feeling and spirit that addresses the total person, his past as well as his present and future. And that incorporates nostalgia—a harkening back to the "Good Old Days", whatever they may be for each individual.

For some it may be those golden days of youth. Days of complete happiness and security. For others it may be former homes or family times and the comfort, pleasure and security those homes or times represented.

Conjure Up Memories. A touch of lace curtain, the turn of a ladder back chair, or a chintz fabric on a sofa are the kinds of things in interiors that may remind us of earlier "homes". They can reawaken dormant memories of people, places and times—in effect, the way things "used to be"—that we cherish and love to recall.

Interiors that in some way stir those memories can also bring back the happiness (or at least suggest the potential) to would-be buyers in your model homes. They suggest comfort. Security. And a link with the past.

In light of the fast-paced tempo of contemporary lifestyle, "homelike" environments in models that evoke nostalgic feelings may be more important than ever in stimulating sales.

How then, does a builder capture this "homelike" nostalgic feeling in his model houses?

It may be as simple as suggesting tradition and heritage with an antique or a reproduction here and there; a piece of period furniture; collections of old things—china, dolls, antique boxes or even records from the good old days stacked on shelves (remember: the "Good Old Days" vary according to age group).

Old family photos, a charming old-fashioned floral print or stripe wallpaper in a room, a lace table cloth, a grandfather clock, a Tiffany lamp, an old fashioned basket filled with pot-pourri . . . all these can be evocative bits of nostalgia.

Even in very contemporary homes there's room for one or two old things which preserve the essence of the past and the strength it may provide us. Remember "Splendor in the Grass" by William Inch? He wrote "Though nothing can bring back the hour of splendor in the grass, of glory in the flower, we will grieve not, yet find strength in what remains behind." In fact, sometimes strong memories are evoked by very small "reminders."

A flower vase of Grandmother's, sitting on our own kitchen table, may bring back to us all the images that prevailed in Grandma's own kitchen when we first gazed upon the vase as a youngster. Also, countless other images, emotions and feelings linked with the vase, with a wonderful Grandmother and the times may be recalled. Since little "reminders" of the nostalgic past are important in people's homes, I really believe they have a limited but very valid place in model homes as well.

"Home"

"The home we first knew
on this beautiful earth,
The friends of our childhood,
the place of our birth,
In the heart's inner chamber
sung always will be,
As the shell ever sings
of its home in the sea"

By Frances Dana Gage
(1808–1884)

Recall a Victorian Mood. Nostalgia really is a love affair with the past, with capturing the flavor and romance of earlier (and perhaps more gentle) times.

It may be inherent in architectural elements—built in or added on later in models. Stained glass windows, wood bannisters, molding, paneling and Victorian fretwork, for example, give us a taste of nostalgia.

Few people today would be comfortable with true Victorian. It was massive, overly ornate and cluttered. But the impression of Victorian in a border of fretwork, for example, is a warm, exciting, romantic look that is easy to live with as well as achieve.

Sometimes evoking nostalgia in model interiors can be as simple as suggesting family activities—family outings, Christmas and other holidays or events that are part of family life. I'm talking about very simple "suggestions" of these things—a picnic basket packed for a day in the country; a piano set with holiday music as if ready for family Christmas caroling; a graduation picture on a dresser.

A good friend of mine once told me that one of the first things she does in a model home is to try to picture just exactly where the Christmas tree would go best. It's important to her! She wants to know that a new home will provide the right environment for special events that make her nostalgic and sentimental about her family.

Use a free hand to stencil or hand-paint colorful designs with tradition. They add personality and help punctuate a theme.

162

The past and present meet gracefully here. An eclectic mix is one way to combine the best of yesterday and today.

163

Certainly, all of us have things we feel sentimental about—belongings we want to be sure will fit comfortably into new houses. My own home is filled with collections of all kinds—dolls, antique tins, stuffed animals, porcelain and glass animals, crystal—and so much more! In every nook, on every shelf and tucked away in corners there are little things that recall in a glimpse (for me, at least) special moments, special friends and special events. I love to be surrounded by these items. Many of them are childlike, fantasy things. They fill my home with a special childlike feeling, even though there are no children. They surround me with reminders of happy times and people I love, and make me feel good!

And I believe home shoppers feel good when they experience the same kind of emotions in models that are evocative of their own "homes"—past and present.

A warm, exciting, romantic Victorian mood exudes from this nostalgia-themed room.

166

Capture Little 'Truths'. Philosophers have written countless lines about "home" and what it means to people. Perhaps the author who suggested that the chief benefit of the house is to "shelter day dreaming . . ." to allow one to "dream in peace" had a point well taken!

But I think Grace Noll Crowell was also right when she wrote these words:

"Home may be near,
Home may be far,
But it is anywhere love
And a few plain household
    treasures are."

Many have spoken of "home" as an atmosphere that recalls early feelings of security and well being (real or imagined) that people spend much of their lives trying to recapture . . . a kind of continuing search for paradise, if you will.

Dictionaries define "home" as "headquarters", "habitat" and "one's place of dwelling or nurturing". And "homelike" is defined as cheerful, cozy, simple, wholesome. In all of these definitions there are, for the builder, words both to build and merchandise by.

Builders and designers in their interior merchandising endeavors, can recall "home" in models to give prospective buyers a sense of the past amid the overwhelming newness of fresh paint, concrete, plaster walls, tinted glass windows, futuristic kitchens and new fangled electronics.

They can do so with style and good taste, and in contemporary settings or traditional ones. It is important to create models that are realistic "homes", that, like the best paintings, address and capture the small truths in our lives—past ones as well as those of the present.

The setting is completely contemporary, but notice how the carved fretwork adds charm.

15

Sprucing Up The Sparkle.

Sometimes a well-merchandised model complex gets messy. Sometimes it gets downright tired—especially in a long-running, multiphase project.

Other times, the thoughtfully-merchandised model simply misses a precise marketing mark.

In this chapter we'll deal with the problems of model merchandising "anemia" and how to put a slow mover back on target—whether it be a simple matter of housekeeping, re-energizing a tired model, or the more complex problem of diagnosing errors and determining what to do about them. In effect, sprucing up the sparkle.

a builder who truly took pride in his project maintained this model to look fresh as new five years after opening!

The results look like new, but the builder saved valuable dollars by using furniture and accessories from an old model complex in this new one.

Keep It Neat. I confess right up front, when it comes to housekeeping, I'm a perfectionist. And a devotee to the theory that there is a place for everything—and everything should be in place. No where does this apply more than in the model home!

In short, I believe good merchandising demands not just good but perfect housekeeping. It's difficult to sell romance and a warm welcome when stains appear in carpeting, table settings disappear, or the Boston fern droops from heat prostration.

Those things may happen in real life, but remember, a model should reflect the homebuyer's dream expectations of how things should be. Since nothings turns off buyers quicker than a messy model, a builder's first rule of thumb should be: Keep everything spotlessly clean and in perfect repair.

Since you'll have little time to attend to the details of housekeeping yourself, make sure the chores are assigned to someone with clear and specific instructions for daily, weekly and monthly routine.

Salesmen might be asked to attend to some of the daily details of "sprucing up"—plant watering, pillow-fluffing and making sure the accessories on the kitchen counter are in place at the day's end, for example.

Right at the beginning of a project, the builder, merchandiser or both can walk through models with salesmen and point out merchandising specifics, housekeeping hints and potential problem areas.

DAILY

- ☐ Fluff pillows
- ☐ Check astrays
- ☐ Straighten bedspreads
- ☐ Dust and vacuum (Daily or 3 to 5 times per week)
- ☐ Clean, wet mop linoleum, tile and other hard floor surfaces (Daily or 3 to 5 times per week)
- ☐ Tidy bathrooms
- ☐ Empty wastebaskets
- ☐ Clean window sills
- ☐ Spot clean windows
- ☐ Check light bulbs
- ☐ Clean entry lights
- ☐ Sweep front walkways
- ☐ Hose off or sweep patios
- ☐ Check outdoor pools/fountains for litter/leaves
- ☐ Clean and add chemicals to pools three times weekly

WEEKLY

- ☐ Water plants (or be sure a plant service does this)
- ☐ Clean and tidy patio furniture, glass top tables, etc.
- ☐ Dust hard-to-reach, out-of-the-way shelves, bookshelves, etc.
- ☐ Clean mirrors and mirrored glass furniture or accessories
- ☐ Polish furniture
- ☐ Drain fountains
- ☐ Clean and dust chandeliers

Housekeeping Checklist

MONTHLY

- ☐ Wash all windows
- ☐ Polish/buff wood flooring
- ☐ Check carpets for stains, spot-clean carpets
- ☐ Professionally clean carpets (Every 3-6 weeks or as needed)

AS NEEDED

- ☐ Resurface wooden floors
- ☐ Strip and seal tile floors
- ☐ Spot-clean or professionally clean upholstery
- ☐ Re-accessorize
- ☐ Replace plants (usually on a monthly basis)
- ☐ Repaint (at least once per year, probably more often)
- ☐ Rewallpaper
- ☐ Professionally clean draperies
- ☐ Restain outdoor decking on patios
- ☐ Replace drains, knobs, hardware items that are damaged or missing
- ☐ Lubricate doors and cabinets to eliminate squeaks, keep them working smoothly

LANDSCAPING

In most large developments, builders will have on staff a regular landscaping crew who will mow lawns, trim bushes and plants, replant and hose off walks and decks on a daily basis.

SIX-MONTH REAPPRAISAL

This is a good time to walk through the model together—builder, merchandiser and possibly sales manager—to review models and re-evaluate what needs to be updated, replaced, repainted or improved. Things to consider will include:

- ☐ Carpets: If very light, do they need to be replaced, now or soon?
- ☐ Walls: Is repainting or re-wallpapering necessary?
- ☐ Accessories: Do they need to be replaced, updated or improved upon in any way?
- ☐ Hardware and light fixtures: What needs to be replaced?
- ☐ Furniture: Is it on target? Does upholstery need cleaning? What about outdoor items; are they in good shape or weather-worn?
- ☐ Landscaping: Has it been well-cared for and kept in prime condition? Have plants become overgrown, or do they interfere with the visual presentation of the home in any way? Are special atriums or gardens within window-view in picture-perfect condition?
- ☐ Miscellaneous: Once again, check drains, knobs, hardware items, cabinets, etc., indoors and out, for items that should be repaired or replaced.

This is the time to press the point that "ashtrays should stay on this table, begonias in the atrium should be watered weekly; and those coffee cups, set there for effect, should not be removed from this serving bar". Salesmen briefed ahead of time will be better able to help you maintain opening day perfection long into the life of a model.

One final word regarding this matter: Even with the best of help—gardeners, housecleaners and the most experienced salesmen or marketing director—often nobody has as critical an eye as the builder when it comes to spotting flaws on his own project.

The burned out track lights, the photo wall with pictures cockeyed, or the spotted clerestory windows may not always catch the eye of salesmen or whoever is making those important house checks. So, I suggest every builder walk through the model complex HIMSELF, at least once a week. And don't hesitate to call the smallest slip-up to someone's attention (no matter how minute!). It will keep your staff on the ball. Chances are, even if you walk through every week with the best people taking care of things, you'll find something out of place or in need of attention every time.

It's also a good idea to schedule walk-throughs with the landscape architect and your interior merchandiser, if you use one, on a regular basis, say every six months or so. This way, your team of professionals can "trouble shoot" or help determine potential trouble spots and suggest solutions.

Older Can Be Better. Understandably, that opening day look is as important—if not more so—weeks, months, even years down the road. A good friend of mine who is marketing director for a large builder told me that he believes the best models don't get older—they get better: landscaping blooms and plants flourish. He's right. Interiors should be re-painted, re-wallpapered, re-carpeted and re-accessorized as need be, right along with those natural exterior "improvements", so that they look better than new.

Large developers generally budget for upkeep, replacement and improvements and establish a regular,

say six-month, reappraisal and maintenance program when they know models will have a long run. This is in addition to daily and weekly housecleaning.

My suggestion to small builders is to plan ahead and budget for cleaning and replacement in your own merchandising programs. As a rule of thumb, you will probably want to budget for such things as carpet replacement (especially if you plan to use a very light carpet), re-painting or wallpapering and re-accessorizing.

No doubt it takes extra dollars to keep a model in perfect condition, but the results will pay the highest return on your initial investment.

Getting Back On Target. Sometimes all the housekeeping in the world isn't enough to help a tired project that somehow misses the mark and falls short of sales appeal.

The warning signs generally are home shopper apathy to the model; poor sales, and negative comments.

Sometimes a stroll through the model to hear how people react helps a builder identify the problems. Comments like "These rooms are too small", "Seems too cluttered", and "These colors are awful" can very easily be changed to:

"The space is used to good advantage here", "I like this arrangement" and "How bright and sunny this room seems" with a few simple changes.

The important first step is to identify exactly <u>what</u> went wrong and <u>where.</u> I remember one very interesting

It's not getting older; it's getting better ... Lots of sunshine and tender loving care have obviously been applied.

A place for everything and everything in it's place. Follow this "golden rule" for results like this!

development—a high-priced project which was brought to my firm for re-do of the interiors. The initial merchandising budget had been large, and everything from wallpaper to furnishings was of the finest quality. However, the total program completely missed the mark. Even though there was an abundance of gorgeous "decorator" items, there was no clearly-defined lifestyle or market direction.

We changed all of that by changing some of the accessories. We replaced a hodge podge of unrelated things with some good artwork—graphics, prints and oils—and a few selected musical instruments and accessories.

The idea was to identify the home as that of a musical family with an interest in art. Once we made those few simple changes and created a family profile, prospects immediately became interested. They pictured the model as the home of a well-educated, cultured family with distinct interests: art and music. The family profile created through new accessorization was directly related to the target market: an upper middle income bracket with conservative ideas, good taste and money to spend on what might be considered important (but not frivolous) items.

What's Hot and What's Not? If your model seems to miss the mark, there are several ways to turn around the merchandising message. You might begin with accessories. First, think in terms of other kinds of merchandising success stories. Remember hoola hoops? They were great until everyone had one and the newness wore off. Skateboards were big sellers for awhile. Then kids discovered roller disco. Nothing's as dead as yesterday's headlines or yesterday's "fad".

And the same is true in model merchandising. Take a look at your own approaches. Are you merchandising dull shower stalls when whirlpool baths are big news? Are you merchandising last fall's colors this spring? Or colors too bold or soft for the current economy? Is your model filled with Mediterranean furniture at a time when country casual is popular, or the Chinese influence is heavy in fashion and interior design?

A San Antonio, Texas, discotheque which my staff designed originally and then redesigned, is living testimony to the fact that trends come and go and merchandising must keep up.

Originally this disco was designed as "Tiffany Palace", with a Victorian carnival feeling. It became THE place for San Antonio's affluent young crowd. However, other discos followed this one, and the fickle crowd was lured away to the "newest" and "latest" each time.

We were called in to design a completely new interior look for the place, this time as Hallelujah Hollywood. We used lots of Hollywood-type art deco, lucite and neon lights. Once again, it became the hottest disco in town, filled to capacity every night, because it was merchandised to sell to market tastes right now!

Merchandising trends in homes are not as volatile as they are in night-time entertainment spots, but the same "keep up with the times" principle applies to models.

If you are experiencing apathy or poor sales, take a realistic look at your product. Does the model look passe? Ask yourself what kind of new, trendy ideas could you introduce to spark up the interior.

Sometimes one very spectacular statement will turn around interest and sales. You might turn a den into a media room with all new electronic TV equipment and games; or add a bright greenhouse room/breakfast nook at the sunny side of a kitchen; carve a skylight in the entry ceiling and install lavish plants and flowers below it. Install a computer as a master switch control or timing device and demonstrate its potential in your model; or, play video-taped messages to buyers on a big screen TV. What's hot and what's not? Answering the query can often help solve sales problems.

Housekeeping is a chore we'd all like to forget. But remember, women will love you for making it look easy. And perfection is something we all strive to achieve. Creating it in your models is a subtle message to buyers that says: "This is the way it could be for you. Take advantage. Live the way you've always wanted to live—right HERE, right now!"

Would you
believe it's
used furniture?
Once again,
he're another
room in which
furniture made
the successful
transition from
old model
to new.

16

Working With The Interior Merchandiser.

This business of merchandising model homes is still a relatively new one. The professional interior merchandiser is somewhat fresh on the scene, although the number of merchandising-oriented interior designers is growing.

Because the "state of the art" is young and developing, all it encompasses may be foreign to many in the shelter-building industry. That may be particularly true with small builders who may have had neither time, budget nor inclination to actively "merchandise" homes as do many builders of large, mass-production developments.

The idea of actually "decorating" model homes—or furnishing them—really gained ground in the 1950s. And the idea of marketing design for specific markets (as opposed to simply creating "pretty places") evolved later in the '70s.

Today, in light of growing competition and increasing sophistication on the part of both builders and home shoppers, I believe interior merchandising's time has arrived.

The COLOR DESIGN ART conference table... here's where the brainstorming begins!

The combination of design aesthetics and people-oriented marketing that is "merchandising" is a natural sales tool with unlimited potential. It is flourishing today because builders are seeking new ways to turn their model home ventures into "adventures" for prospective buyers. A growing number of contemporary home buyers want to "shop" and experience home environments much as they might try on new clothes, or test drive a new car before the final purchase.

Along with the evolution of interior merchandising, builders are asking how and where to find the professional interior merchandiser, and finally, how to work with these professionals.

I wrote this book as a do-it-yourself merchandising guideline for builders who may want to supervise the merchandising job themselves. But if you decide to hire or consult an outside professional, the materials in this chapter are designed to help you make the most of your working relationship, and ultimately, create more exciting homes and reap maximum sales.

In order to do so, merchandising plans must be organized. I've found that the best programs usually result from two key factors:

Who would guess it's a sales office! The point is, it's not stuffy or "official", it's a place that puts prospects at ease.

(1) The builder determines exactly what he wants to accomplish in his models—what kind of a sales pitch he wants to make.

(2) He tells the professional interior merchandiser—if he chooses to work with one—exactly what he expects, then works closely with that pro until the results are produced.

A successful builder with whom I have worked frequently had one of the most professional philosophies or approaches to merchandising his homes that I've come across. I have outlined it here:

(1) First and foremost this builder believes in good architecture in his initial product.

(2) From the beginning, he sits down with the professional interior merchandiser and goes over floor plans.

(3) He holds joint meetings at the beginning of every project with all consultants—designer/merchandiser, architect, public relations and advertising consultants, etc.

(4) The builder visits the site with consultants early.

(5) He provides the merchandiser with a marketing overview of the development.

(6) He sets up timetables.

(7) And follows through!

(8) He has an organized, professional team.

(9) He is enthusiastic and motivates his consultants and salesmen.

(10) He asks lots of questions of the designer/merchandiser and gives feedback to their questions.

(11) And he is totally involved in the merchandising process.

Shop For A Pro. Many competent interior designers can put furniture and accessories into a home attractively, but it takes a designer with a marketing/merchandising "sense" to develop lifestyle environments through interior design.

For builders who decide to consult a professional interior merchandiser, my advice is to seek the best and do it early! Ideally, the individual or firm will be able to offer you invaluable ideas from the preliminary plan stage and on. Here are some other guidelines to help you select a competent pro:

(1) Investigate First.

Your best bet is to shop the developments of colleagues. Solicit their recommendations, and check out the reputations as well as finished products of firms or individuals recommended to you. See for yourself how they operate.

You should look for proof of experience, reputation and competence in two areas: merchandising and performance. Remember that an accomplished interior designer may or may not be experienced in model home merchandising. An interior merchandiser is market oriented. Competence in budgeting, or following your budget requirements, are also areas of expertise you should look for in the professional you choose to consult.

References may help you to determine if your prospects are experienced in coordination of all aspects of merchandising as well as design.

(2) Ask For A Plan.

A preliminary merchandising plan should give you a clear idea of what the individual or firm will do in terms of:

- Furnishings
- Color
- Layout
- Built-ins
- Accesories
- Wrappings
- Standard and upgrade materials

It should include a time plan for decoration of models and sales office and a post-opening evaluation or critique. A full merchandising package would include critique of the floor plans; coordination with architect and landscape architect; coordination of production color, and recommendations on standard and upgrade wall and floor coverings, fixture and counter top materials.

In addition, the merchandiser will create those specific "family profiles" for each model before the mechanics of the interior design are implemented.

(3) Know What It Costs

Merchandising packages vary in cost. While some companies favor a fee based on square footage, I believe the best plans, from a builder's standpoint, break down specific costs such as furnishings, wallcoverings, labor, intallation, etc.

Be sure that your pro has sound marketing reasons for plans and proposals, particularly any that may be foreign to your market. If preliminary plans call for vignettes, for example, be sure vignetting is right in light of your specific market population and product.

(4) The Final Critique.

A critique or evaluation after the merchandised models have been completed allows for refinement or correction by both you and the merchandiser to assure the best package for your money.

You may also want to ask your merchandiser to include a specific maintenance plan for continued upkeep of the "opening day" look of your models.

(5) Professional Help On A Shoestring Budget.

If a small budget limits your options of hiring a full-time professional merchandiser you can always seek professional advice on a limited, consulting basis.

The professional may be able to give you, in a few consulting sessions billed at an hourly fee, invaluable advice you can implement yourself.

Suggestions on dealing with floor plan problems, small spaces, special architectural features or elevations, theming, color and market orientation can often put you on the right track toward optimum sales, or help you avoid pitfalls. A professional also can advise you on sales-effective decisions for standard features, fixtures, counter top materials and upgrading (when and when not to do so).

When sales are slow, a consultation with a professional merchandiser may help turn the faltering development into a successful one. Often it's as simple as making changes in accessories or furniture items.

The dollars you invest in a solid merchandising program orchestrated by a competent professional almost always pays off in sales. You may end up paying more for a merchandising package than say, an agreement with a local furniture retailer or design center, but you'll ideally reap greater benefits in terms of traffic, sales and identity of your firm and your product.

What To Expect From The Pro. In order to get the most professional results and your money's worth on an agreement with an interior merchandiser, you'll want to know that your professional package covers all aspects of the interior job from planning to installation.

Here's an outline of major points you may want to be sure are covered in your own agreements!

The Complete Package

1. Critique of Plans. Your professional should view the site, study your competition and the surrounding neighborhood. Then meet with the architect and other consultants early in the planning process to critique plans and coordinate objectives.
2. Formal Presentation. After the merchandiser has studied your project, set a date for a formal presentation (or outline) from the pro that includes:
   - Layouts of each plan
   - Color boards, or depiction of color schemes and fabrics
   - Photographs of furniture selected
   - Wall elevations and architectural built-in features
   - Drapery treatment
   - Wall coverings selected
   - Sketches of specific designed areas
   - Flooring and finish material samples
   - Locations for live plants
3. Finishing Schedule. Following approval of the design plan, your merchandiser should provide a finishing schedule which specifies such things as paint color or finishes, placement of wall coverings, and other details. When dry walling is completed at the models, the merchandiser may mark walls for coverings and review plans for execution of the built-ins.
4. Installation. Includes supervision of all aspects of installation.
5. Follow-up Inspection.

Color boards can be a part of the interior merchandiser's presentation that later become a builder's tool.

191

17

Get The Most Out of Your Merchandising Dollar. The fear that model merchandising means skyrocketing costs has caused many home builders to shy away from commitment to a sales-oriented merchandising program. They argue that they can't afford a professional merchandising package.

But nothing could be less true. Model merchandising IS cost-effective when the home builder is familiar with the techniques that get him <u>the most for his merchandising dollar.</u>

This chapter will deal with cost-effective, "dollar-and-cents" details of merchandising, such as:

- Planning and budgeting ahead.
- The "Merchandising" dollar vs. the "Decorating" dollar.
- Maximizing the investment.
- What to expect in return.

Merchandising takes in the <u>entire space</u>, without emphasizing one singular aspect of design. It's spreading the dollar around for <u>total impact</u>.

Plan and Budget Ahead. There are no "quick-and-easy" or fixed formulas for budgeting model merchandising costs. Some home builders base their budgets on the "one percent rule". That is, as a guideline, they allocate one percent of the total sales price of all units in a development to model interior design. This guideline works well for large projects but doesn't really apply effectively to a small builder's projects. The investment you make on smaller projects will depend on the specifics of each model or model complex.

That means, before getting down to price tags or budgets, you've got to ask and answer some pertinent and specific merchandising questions, such as:

- What are your sales objectives?
- Who's the market?
- How many units will you build?
- At what prices?
- What's the economy doing?
- And what's the competition doing?

Once you've addressed those considerations, you should have a good idea of what kind of impact you will want—and need—to make in your own merchandising program.

The next step is to talk to a professional merchandiser; in fact, talk to several. The comparisons will give you a good idea of realistic costs and what you can expect to budget for your own plan.

Then allocate the funds right at the beginning of your building program. You may decide later not to spend all you've budgeted, but at least you'll have planned ahead.

And while your're planning— plan ahead for inflation, too. It's particularly important when the gap between budgeting and actual implementation of your model program is going to be a big one—say six months or more. Because budget and costs of things do change, the best inflation-fighting weapon you have is to be cost-conscious at the planning stage and to make allowances for inflationary spurts. Then you can grin and bear it if, and when, price tags spiral upwards. It's easier to bear the cost crunch if you've been wise in planning.

How The Dollar Is Spent. Many a builder has spent a bundle on "decorating" models only to find that the resulting interiors have all the appeal of a furniture store window but little of the warmth of a "home". The fact is, "merchandising a home" environment need not necessarily cost more than "decorating".

HOWEVER, the money will be spent in different ways in merchandising programs. Here's how: If we took two identical model homes with identical interior design budgets, it would not be unusual for the merchandising and the decorating purchasing priorities to differ as shown on the following charts:

The main difference between decorating and merchandising is that the merchandising dollar is allocated to create total impact on the most likely buyers. Accessories, built-ins and wallcoverings generally receive greater emphasis. Furnishings won't be as expensive as in a decorating plan, but your purpose is not to impress prospects with expensive furniture items. The bottom line for the merchandising plan is sales. And sales are generated by a livable, inviting environment which turns on prospects to the lifestyle your models offer.

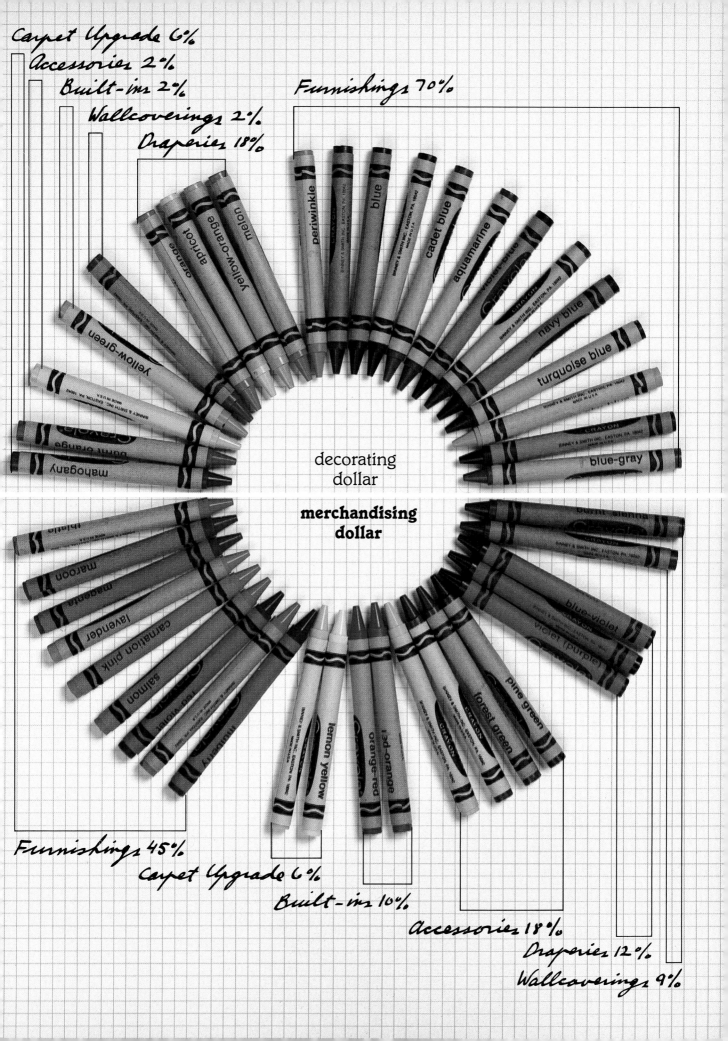

Carpet Upgrade 6%

Accessories 2%

Built-ins 2%

Wallcoverings 2%

Draperies 18%

Furnishings 70%

decorating dollar

merchandising dollar

Furnishings 45%

Carpet Upgrade 6%

Built-ins 10%

Accessories 18%

Draperies 12%

Wallcoverings 9%

You Get What You Pay For. You may or may not find that estimates from a professional merchandiser seem higher than an arrangement with a furniture store or a small interior decorator. If you are concerned about cost, check over the professional merchandiser's proposed plan and see how it proposes that your dollars be spent. At the same time, keep in mind these factors concerning budget:

1. You're dealing with a specialist. As a result you can, and should expect a better job for your money.

2. What may seem like more at first, may cost less in the end in terms of faster sales and premium prices for your homes as the result of quality merchandising.

To make sure you're getting the most for your money, there are some dependable signs you can watch for to alert you when programs are going astray. If the merchandiser or decorator isn't prepared for a pre-scheduled presentation or presents only a partial package, it's time to ask some questions. Or, if a project is running behind schedule, over budget or if secondary rooms are skimped over in favor of expensive decor in primary living spaces—the completed model may not be cost-effective.

Maximize Your Investment. Whether you implement your own program or use a professional, here are some simple ways to maximize your investment in a merchandising program:

1. Take fullest advantage of the professional's experience at the earliest time. Your pro can then critique preliminary plans to ensure they function well for furniture layout.

2. Given plenty of advance ordering/purchasing time the professional generally can provide better quality merchandise at less cost through advance order discounts. This can provide you with genuine savings.

3. Early communication between merchandiser and landscape architect enables coordination of indoor floor coverings and landscape paving materials that give you the best results for your money (and avoids costly mistakes).

4. And finally: <u>Pamper your purchasing agent!</u> This is often the forgotten person but one of the most important staff members on a builder's team when it comes to stretching merchandising dollars. Here's why:

· By coordinating efforts of merchandiser and purchasing agent early-on, you can remove limitations on the jobs of each.

· The merchandiser isn't limited by having to devise an interior scheme around existing entry tiles, carpet and wall coverings. These can be customized for each home by the designer but ordered through the purchasing agent to save on costs.

· And your purchasing agent can benefit from the professional merchandiser's familiarity with new products, alternative manufacturers and quality-comparable lines when ordering standard fixtures. A slight upgrading of kitchen tile, or hardware and lighting fixtures, for example, or a switch to another manufacturer as recommended by the experienced interior merchandiser may add just the subtle sizzle a buyer is looking for in your homes.

What To Expect In Return. Most builders can anticipate recapturing a generous portion of the cost of merchandising model interiors when models are closed out. It's realistic to anticipate a 100 percent return on your architectural built-ins, wall coverings and draperies. A return of fifty-cents on the dollar is realistic for furnishings, though sometimes you can expect more.

In the Southern California market in particular, developers have received more than 100 percent return on their investments. In this market many buyers frankly expect total merchandising. They are often eager to buy a merchandised model "as is" and will go the extra cost for the total environment package.

Whether prospects buy your finished models for 100 percent return on your dollar or not, the investment, in time, effort and dollars for good merchandising, almost always pays for itself in sales results in the developments. There's no magic involved. It's a matter of effective budgeting and planning.

18

The 'Model' Model.

It's difficult to describe THE perfect model house, since perfection, like beauty, is measured in the eyes of the beholder. But, I'm going to give it a try.

There's no single 'perfection' formula I can prescribe, for we know that the expectations of home buyers are sure to vary. The 25 to 35 year-old buyer, with two kids and a dog, seeking The Perfect House in the suburbs will have ideals far different from those of two sophisticated singles sharing the investment in a city townhome, or empty nesters with an eye to retirement in a marina-front condo.

Obviously the perfect model home is not a static thing, but a living, changing ideal that varies with markets, bank balances and personal aspirations. However, I do believe there are standards of perfection that span consumer categories and home price ranges. And I'm firmly convinced

attention to detail and a sense of careful concern shine through in the best model homes.

that, barring some unlikely situation that would reduce all homes to standard uniformity, there will always be a demand for homes that portray personality and exemplify the best to be had at every price range.

The task of architect, builder, decorator and merchandiser at every level is to provide the best. And, as I've stated so many times, I don't mean the best in interiors simply from an aesthetic viewpoint, but from a lifestyle viewpoint as well.

That really is what those of us involved in the shelter industry today must sell. Not structures, not buildings, not "four bedrooms/two baths/and family room" . . . but lifestyles . . . better lifestyles for people who want and demand more than shelter. The promise of every model home must be a better tomorrow—achieveable, affordable and available right now, right here, in this home!

Dreams, enthusiasm and excitement sell homes. Mediocrity, repetition and lacklustre presentations do not.

Exercise. Active! Young. The lifestyle is self-explanatory in this secondary bedroom.

Why They Buy. I have merchandised more than 1,500 individual model homes in some 400 developments across the country and I've had the opportunity to talk and work with builders and buyers in a variety of market situations. I've learned merchandising maxims no school could teach! In observing home shoppers over the years I've also gained insight into why people buy. They choose a home for an assortment of obvious reasons such as price and number of bedrooms.

But most important, they buy to fulfill a sense of self-worth. A sense of self-distinction and achievement that a particular home, like a designer label or the status appeal of a distinctive automobile, imparts to its owner. In homes, the interior can be the "label" that gives your buyer the feeling of buying "up" and increasing his self-esteem and prestige in doing so.

Sensual and aesthetic satisfaction in the environment of a home also induces people to buy. This is why the selection of colors, wrappings, accessories, the scale and proportion of items used, and the harmonious arrangement of the total presentation have become finely honed skills. Buyers who are unsure of how a house will "look" and "live" or of how to create a tasteful environment themselves, get a clear understanding of exactly "how" when a home is well merchandised. And they receive the accompanying security that they are making a tasteful choice.

Every builder, large or small, can meet the aesthetic considerations of good design and good merchandising that help generate buyer appeal by addressing the following list of "essentials". Remember, the essentials apply whether you're building a few homes or a few hundred!

The Twelve Essential Elements of Model Home Merchandising

1. ENVIRONMENT—The environment is a model's "personality", created by the architecture, special features and special arrangement of the floor plan. Make it inviting.

2. MOOD—The mood is the "feeling" created within the space through decor, to enhance the environment. It showcases the home, not the decorator!

3. MARKET APPEAL—The direction of decor should be targeted toward a specific market. Colors and all interior items are chosen with this key buyer market in mind.

4. COLOR—Color theme should be balanced, geared to the market, and carried out throughout the entire model home.

5. LAYOUT AND TRAFFIC PATTERN—These should contribute to easy "flow" of traffic. They are designed to move prospects through the home in the most inviting way. (But never use ropes or plastic runners!)

6. LIGHTING—Highlights the best features of architecture and decor, lends personality and interest, and focuses attention on special features.

7. FLOOR AND WALLCOVERINGS—Are coordinated with all colors and patterns in other surface coverings. Floor covering color is usually the major color in the home.

8. ACCESSORIES—They add character, describe the lifestyle a home affords and the types of people who might live there.

9. FURNITURE—Enhances the lifestyle treatment and compliments the market, but is never overwhelming or too expensive for the market.

10. WINDOW TREATMENT—Helps set the stage, highlights views and extends the outdoors in.

11. PLANTS—Add realism, life and enthusiasm to decor. (Never use phoney plants!)

12. BUILT-IN FEATURES—Bookcases, wetbars, shelving, wall molding and trim, et. al., maximize space, demonstrate potential use of space, and contribute strong focal points of interest.

An obvious traffic pattern is created by furniture layout. It's important to "guide" shoppers this way...

and, to introduce
focal points
like the
built-in above.

The sum of the parts makes the perfect whole...

It's a skillful combination of the right accessories, furniture, surface coverings and window treatments.

Commit To The Best. The 12 essential elements of merchandising are basic to every model program. But in addition to these very tangible items, I believe there are eight challenges facing the builder, large or small, who would create the perfect model home. The first is to COMMIT TO THE BEST in your merchandising program.

Unfortunately, many model homes that could be memorable fall short of perfection because the builder or developer simply does not commit himself to full-fledged merchandising once past the construction stage.

These builders forget that selling is merchandising— whether you've got a single home or acres of them. They create cookie cutter model interiors that simply repeat what the competition is doing down the line, and bore home shoppers to tears in doing so.

The difference between the hotel-motel monotony of many of these homes, and the "sellers"—the homes that grab buyers with their inherent enthusiasm—begins with the enthusiasm of the builder himself.

I've watched builders of successful projects and seen qualities they have in common. They display greater merchandising expertise than their competitors, but they also are willing to put in extra effort to produce quality, and never settle for second best. The results are not only sales but increased esteem in the industry and among buyers.

These builders also start with a "Do it all the way or don't do it at all", philosophy. A builder's most blatant flaw is to do less than a 100 percent job.

Secondly, their own commitment is imparted to everyone on the team. Perfection has to start with the ideals of the builder in charge, and then be carried out by an experienced merchandiser or merchandising program and be filtered right down through all staff to the salesman in the models.

Salesmen should be made aware of the merchandising elements that make a home unique and special. Whether they be built-ins, large pantrys, storage space, or futuristic appliances, the buyer isn't going to know about them, or appreciate them, if presented in a lukewarm fashion by disinterested or half-hearted salesmen.

When it comes down to bottom line, it's attention to detail that separates memorable models from ordinary ones.

Note how family room fun is reflected in the mirrored miniature train center above. Below, patterned detail is beautifully but simply repeated in fabric and wall covering.

Generate Excitement. The second challenge is to GENERATE EXCITEMENT in the model home. The best models are entertaining. Pure show biz. A grand place to visit—and a grand place to live besides. It happens with color, elements of surprise and delight, clever use of space, entertaining ways with furniture and appliances—in short, visual effectiveness and plenty of fun zones. Books are on shelves, everything is warm and cozy. It all comes together to welcome <u>and</u> amuse.

There's nothing timid or shy about the best merchandising jobs, from first impressions on!

The third challange is to CREATE A MEMORABLE FIRST IMPRESSION. Hands down, there should be nothing ho-hum about what the buyer sees first—usually entries or living rooms. You've got to seize immediate attention and stir up emotional involvement on impact.

Warmth, hominess, romance, excitement and drama are the kinds of emotions buyers should experience when they walk in the door. One way to create a memorable first impression is to focus on a "focal point" such as an atrium. Treat it like the centerpiece on a table. It may not be a functional space, but it will make your model memorable, add to the visual effectiveness of the decor and to lasting favorable impressions.

The fourth challenge is a point I'm guilty of repeating to distraction. But nonetheless I'll say it again because it's that important! ADDRESS THE TARGET MARKET'S EXPECTATIONS.

A perfect model meets market demand in presentation, class and quality of materials. It's one thing to walk into a model complex and appreciate the cosmetics and professionalism of design. But it's quite another if the results ultimately address the personality and pocketbook of the prospective buyer. The best models address that person directly and make him <u>want</u> to buy!

Rooms To Groom. After the entry or living room or whatever the eye sees first, challenge number five—is to HIGHLIGHT THE MOST IMPORTANT ROOMS. They are:

• Master suites—Always abide by the Cleopatra syndrome—make them as glamorous as possible!

• Kitchens and baths—These are the show-case rooms. You can merchandise the most current trends here, and there's a steady stream of new and irresistible products to help you do it to the utmost!

• Family rooms—People like to "look" in living rooms, but they live in family rooms. Thus, they should be comfortable and serve many uses. In particular, provide areas for family entertainment.

• Dining and eating areas—They're as essential as bread and jam to tea time. People desire some formality to the ritual of eating. If dining rooms and eating nooks are not built into floor plans formally, they should be merchandised later. Show exactly where tables will fit.

208

Start From The Foundation Up. You can't create a perfect model unless you start with a good foundation. Challenge number six is: DESIGN EXCELLENCE INTO YOUR ARCHITECTURAL PLANS. You can't turn a poorly designed home into a perfect model without the basics.

A good foundation means well-planned floor plans. And here the word again is quality not quantity! Big is not necessarily synonymous with the best. But the best is always space-conscious. That means making maximum use of limited space with special features such as vaulted ceilings to help expand visual dimension.

Surprise And Delight. Challenge number seven is: MERCHANDISE AN ELEMENT OF SURPRISE. Surprise may be delivered through special attention to "forgotten" spaces such as patios and decks. These are ideal for adding valuable square footage in cold as well as warm climates. Builders who don't sell these areas may be missing out on a great way to beef up merchandising.

Another "forgotten" space is the basement. Instead of leaving it undone, you can surprise prospects by capitalizing on what's in vogue . . . a finished basement is an American dream. So merchandise it!

Whimsy, fantasy and a few child-like elements are "surprise" qualities I've said should be incorporated into every model home in some small way. Toys and children's books and their accompanying fantasy were never meant to be the exclusive property of children! A touch of whimsy here and there to put smiles on faces, to remind buyers to stop, relax, fantasize, and laugh has never been known to prevent a sale!

My own home is strictly an adult home, but in addition to antiques and contemporary art, I've filled it with a legion of toys, collections of animals, dolls, porcelain figures, books and whimsical knick knacks with childlike quality. I firmly believe in these touches of fantasy to put people at ease, make them set aside serious matters, relax and enjoy themselves. I've seen it work in my own home and in model homes as well.

A fanciful heart shaped mirror that I've used at least 27 times for this purpose has been one of the most successful accessories I've ever used in models. A doll or whimiscal picture may work equally as well.

The resources for touches of childlike accessories are unlimited, but you rarely find these happy notes in model homes, perhaps because serious minded builders and decorators too often forget to stop and enjoy themselves or encourage customers to do so, too.

Think about Tomorrow. Finally, the ultimate challenge, challenge number eight is: THINK ABOUT TOMORROW. Ideals of perfection will continue to change just as markets and trends change. And, therefore, merchandising philosophy must transcend the short range and consider the long range.

Manufacturers constantly are altering their lines, modifying inventories, announcing a new space-aged wonder or faithfully reproducing a time-honored classic.

What's here today may be gone tomorrow. The basic elements of design and merchandising as COLOR IT HOME explains them, will always apply. But we must be ready to apply these basics to new thinking and innovative ideas.

To our good fortune, we have better tools for our trade than ever before. And what looms on the horizon is even more inspiring. Computers. Advanced electronics. Labor and energy-saving technology. All of this to meet the demands of a sophisticated buying public and to motivate our own creative efforts.

We are entering an age of adventure. Homebuilders and merchandisers will have opportunity to implement changes that transcend what has happened in the entire history of shelter-building.

But as we go forward we must bring along with us the time-proven appendages of the profession. We must proceed with love and care lest we fail in our goal of interpreting dreams and translating them into viable lifestyles and saleable homes.

The 'model' model is a blending of the best: balance, contrast, interesting detail, shape, texture, color and pattern.

Credits

Ponderosa Homes
Project: **Los Tesoros** Photographer:
Leland Lee Page:7,13, 14,15, 16, 17,19,
22, 39,46-47, 48-49,52, 60, 66, 67, 79
90,92, 98-99, 108-109, 112-113, 124,
132-133, 146, 154, 192, 210.

Project: **Bonita** Photographer: **Leland Lee**
Page:176-177, 199, 203, 204, 205, 77.

Project: **Park Paseo** Photographer:
Leland Lee Page:28,31,35.

Roger C. Werbel, Inc.
Project: **Villa Verde** Photographer:
Leland Lee Page: 10, 58-59, 81, 88-89,
126-127,130-131, 162-163, 164-165,
186-187.

Countyline Communities
Project: **Fox Run** Photographer:**Leland
Lee** Page: 11, 61, 172-173,182-183.

AVCO Community Developers
Project: **Heritage** Photographer: **Leland
Lee** Page: 12.

Project: **Heritage** Photographer: **Mike
Muckley** Page: 20, 3, 5, 118, 116.

Pulte Homes
Project: **Villa de Paz** Photographer:
Leland Lee Page:178-179.

The Gunston Hall Company, Inc.
Project: **Pointe Quissett** Photographer:
Leland Lee Page: 19, 28, 29, 30, 31,
32, 33, 34, 35.

M.J. Brock & Sons
Project: **Brock Homes/Saugus**
Photographer: **Leland Lee** Page: 10,
166-167.

Valencia Corporation
Project: **Sunrise** Photographer: **Leland
Lee** Page: 13, 138, 140-141, 143,
144-145, 204.

Irvine Pacifica
Project: **Rancho San Joaquin**
Photographer: **Leland Lee** Page: 28,
33, 34, 120.

Project: **Woodbridge Gables**
Photographer: **Leland Lee** Page 68-69,
119, 120, 150-151, 156, 168-169.

Project: **Harbor View Knoll**
Photographer: **Leland Lee** Page 135

Metropolitan Development
Project: **Country Vista** Photographer:
Leland Lee Page: 50-51.

Trend Setter Homes of Florida
Project: **La Foret** Photographer: **Leland
Lee** Page: 55,56, 106-107, 115, 123.

Shapell Industries
Project: **Presidio Place** Photographer:
Leland Lee Page: 64, 75.

Project: **Monarch Hill** Photographer:
Leland Lee Page 100-101.

Bren Company
Project: **El Sobrante** Photographer: **Robb
Miller** Page: 70,72, 73, 84, 207.

Project: **Glen Cove** Photographer: **Robb
Miller** Page: 72,73, 74, 86, 148, 203.

Kohler Bath
Photographer: **Hedrick- Blessing**
Page: 104, 110-111.

Beverly's
Project: **Master Bedroom** Photographer:
Leland Lee Page: 95.

Project: **Garden Room** Photographer:
Leland Lee Page: 96.

Project: **Guest Bedroom** Photographer:
Leland Lee Page:102-103.

Knoell Homes
Project: **Knoell East** Photographer:
Leland Lee Page: 170.

D & S Company
Project: **Canyon Village** Photographer:
Leland Lee Page: 201.